After the Suicide

Helping the Bereaved to Find a Path from Grief to Recovery

Kari Dyregrov, Einar Plyhn and Gudrun Dieserud

Foreword by John R. Jordan

Jessica Kingsley *Publishers*
London and Philadelphia

Figure 11.1 on p.152 is reproduced by permission of M. Stroebe

First published in 2010 in Norwegian by
Abstrakt Forlag AS, Oslo, Norway, as *Etter selvmordet – veien videre*

This edition first published in English in 2012
by Jessica Kingsley Publishers
116 Pentonville Road
London N1 9JB, UK
and
400 Market Street, Suite 400
Philadelphia, PA 19106, USA

www.jkp.com

Library of Congress Cataloging in Publication Data
Dyregrov, Kari.
  [Etter selvmordet. English]
  After the suicide : helping the bereaved to find a path from grief to
recovery / Kari Dyregrov, Einar Plyhn and Gudrun Dieserud.
      p. cm.
  "First published in 2010 in Norwegian by Abstrakt Forlag AS, Oslo, Norway,
as Etter selvmordet : veien videre."
  Includes bibliographical references and index.
  ISBN 978-1-84905-211-5 (alk. paper)
  1. Suicide victims--Family relationships. 2. Suicide--Psychological
aspects. 3. Bereavement. I. Plyhn, Einar, 1951- II. Dieserud, Gudrun, 1944-
III. Title.
  HV6545.D97 2012
  362.28'3--dc23
                                      2011018980

British Library Cataloguing in Publication Data
A CIP catalogue record for this book is available from the British Library

ISBN 978 1 84905 211 5
eISBN 978 0 85700 445 1

Printed and bound in Great Britain

Contents

Foreword

After the Suicide: Helping the Bereaved to Find a Path from Grief to Recovery is an excellent book, one that is sure to make a significant contribution to the body of literature helping the bereaved after suicide. Kari Dyregrov, Einar Plyhn, and Gudrun Dieserud have given both suicide survivors (the term used in North America for people who are grieving after the loss of a loved one to suicide), and those who seek to help them, a rich and relevant resource from which to draw. Based on Kari Dyregrov's long and productive history as a bereavement researcher (where she has focused particularly on the role of social interaction between the bereaved and their social networks), this book is firmly grounded in empirical research that enriches the information and advice that is offered. Yet despite its solid scientific foundation, the book is eminently readable: clear, simple, and comprehensive in its coverage of the experience of losing a loved one to suicide. Moreover, the ideas presented are beautifully illustrated with quotations from suicide survivors themselves, a feature that adds to the ability of the text to speak directly to those who are searching for wisdom about coming to terms with this most difficult of traumatic losses. In addition to Dyregrov, the co-authors also include a person bereaved by suicide himself, and an individual with expertise in public health. This outstanding blending of scientific expertise, clinical acumen, and personal understanding of the suicide bereaved marks *After the Suicide* as unique in the plethora of books that offer guidance to suicide survivors.

After the Suicide begins with two helpful overview chapters that give the reader an overview of grief, laying out some of the reasons why grief after suicide is different than grief after other types of losses, and exploring the epidemiology and history of social attitudes towards suicide. These introductory pieces serve to pave the way for the next four chapters, which plunge into the heart of the experience of losing someone to suicide with vivid descriptions of the reactions of suicide survivors in their own words. These chapters are also underpinned by frequent citation of the research literature on the reactions of the suicide bereaved. The content is sure to resonate with anyone who has lived through the experience of losing someone close to them to suicide, or anyone who has worked extensively with the suicide bereaved. The chapters serve as excellent explanations of grief and trauma responses, both of which are common for suicide survivors. In particular, Chapter 5 provides a valuable synopsis of many of the effects of a suicide that are likely to be more prominent for survivors, and equally likely to be underestimated by the social networks who surround the bereaved. Lastly, to the author's credit, they have included an excellent chapter on the impact of suicide on child and adolescent survivors, something lacking in many books written for survivors.

The next section of the *After the Suicide* consists of four chapters that offer tremendous assistance to suicide survivors who are looking for practical guidance on how to cope with the potentially devastating impact of suicide on individuals and families. In a contribution that reflects the particular research background and recognized expertise of Kari Dyregrov, these chapters provide concrete advice to various people in the social networks of the suicide bereaved who seek to offer comfort and support in the healing process. The chapters address friends and family, other bereaved in survivor support groups, and professional bereavement caregivers (clergy, funeral professionals, mental health professionals, etc.). This distinctive feature of the book is unique in the breadth and depth of its coverage of the responses needed from social networks to facilitate recovery in the bereaved. It is a wonderful example of how good research can be translated into clear and practical advice for the bereaved and their caregivers. The unifying theme of the value of openness on the part of the bereaved about their needs is directly in accord with the experience of most clinicians who have worked extensively with survivors (including my own), and of the suicide bereaved themselves. *After the Suicide* presents clinical wisdom that has been validated by the excellent research of Dr Dyregrov, and now with the publication of this book, has been expertly translated into information that will be of direct help to those who support the suicide bereaved.

Lastly, *After the Suicide* concludes with two marvelous chapters: one on post-traumatic growth after suicide, and the other on contemporary theories that help the reader to make sense of the mysterious phenomenon that is suicide. Like the rest of the book, the chapter on post-traumatic growth offers an up-to-date understanding of contemporary bereavement theory. It provides the reader with the hope that, even in the face of a catastrophic loss such as suicide, the bereaved can not only recover, but can grow in resilience and wisdom. Likewise, the final chapter, titled 'Why Suicide?', offers the reader a thoughtful and sophisticated review of a modern psychological (though not a neurobiological) understanding of the factors that may contribute to suicide. Throughout, it appropriately emphasizes that suicide must be understood as a kind of 'perfect storm', a coming together of multiple and complex elements that create the psychological conditions that make suicide likely.

In sum, *After the Suicide* is a superb book for those who are bereaved by suicide, for those who wish to help them, and for those whose professional work leads them to walk the difficult journey with survivors. I have specialized in working with suicide bereavement in my own practice for many years, and yet I learned a great deal from reading this fine book. It weaves together scientific knowledge of bereavement and trauma, the personal narratives of survivors themselves, and a deep compassion and understanding of the pain that suicide leaves behind to create an outstanding resource for the suicide bereaved around the world. Bravo!

John R. Jordan, PhD, FT, psychologist
and Founder and former Director of the Family Loss Project, USA

Preface

This book is the result of a close collaboration between three authors and a number of individuals bereaved by suicide. Although the authors have actively commented and worked on one another's texts, the chief author of this book is without any doubt Kari Dyregrov.

The initiative for the book came from Einar Plyhn. Finding no suitable literature after he personally experienced bereavement by suicide, he decided, as a publisher, to attempt to produce the book he had felt a need for at that time. He contacted Kari Dyregrov at the Norwegian Institute of Public Health/Center for Crisis Psychology, who immediately agreed to take part in writing such a book. Kari involved Einar in the writing process. Eventually, Gudrun Dieserud at the Norwegian Institute of Public Health was also invited to contribute as an author.

An early draft of the manuscript was sent to people bereaved by suicide and to professionals, and these individuals made a number of valuable comments. Although we have not followed up on all the suggestions, our readers have made an important contribution to the final result. A large thank you to everyone!

Kari Dyregrov was awarded a writer's grant from the Norwegian Non-Fiction Writers and Translators Association to write the book. A large thank you also to the Freedom of Expression Foundation, Oslo, and the Norwegian Foundation for Health and Rehabilitation, which have generously supported the work on the book and the publication itself, and to LEVE, The Norwegian Organization for Suicide Survivors, who allowed us to apply for funding from the Norwegian Foundation for Health and Rehabilitation through them as a user organization. Thank you as well to the Norwegian Institute of Public Health for inspiring support. Finally, we would like to thank Diane Oatley for her work on the English translation.

We hope that those bereaved by suicide will find help towards recovery in this book and that it can contribute to making the professional helpers and social networks of the bereaved better prepared to provide assistance.

Kari Dyregrov, Einar Plyhn and Gudrun Dieserud
Bergen and Oslo, December 2009

To the Reader

A BOOK OF HELP

This book has come about through a collaboration between individuals bereaved by suicide and professionals. We hope that it will provide inspiration and knowledge for those professional helpers and the networks of family and friends of those bereaved by suicide as well as the bereaved themselves.

Many people bereaved by suicide have looked for literature that can help. No book can replace human support and care, but knowledge is always a resource, because it illustrates what common reactions to suicide are, the type of support and care that is important for the bereaved, and how relief measures can best be organized.

The aim of the book is first and foremost to provide understanding about people who have personally experienced the impact of a suicide and how they can be best supported, but we also hope that the book will offer advice to those who may be a part of a bereaved person's support network, or to bereaved people themselves.

The book presents relevant research findings about suicide and those bereaved by suicide, about common reactions to suicide and how friends, family, the school, the workplace and professionals can address the great challenges that arise and how they can help. The book contains a number of testimonies from those bereaved by suicide, which illuminate, exemplify or provide further depth to the subject matter, and many readers will recognize their experiences. The names used in the testimonies have been changed and the quotations are used with the permission of the bereaved.

We have endeavoured to make the book easily accessible, among other ways by avoiding unnecessarily technical language. All references to research and literature are in the form of endnotes.

We have also included website links to support groups or resource communities that can provide assistance in connection with a suicide. The research projects that are mentioned in the book are given a brief presentation in the Useful Resources section.

HOW TO READ THIS BOOK

People bereaved by suicide who have a need for knowledge and information immediately following a suicide, will perhaps initially search for specific themes and only be capable of reading more at a later date. Professionals who are unfamiliar with the subject matter will perhaps wish to read the entire text in a more logical structure – from the first chapter to the last. The book can therefore be read in its entirety, from cover to cover, or little by little and in sections, both back to front or diagonally. In order to make it possible to read each chapter independently, some repetition has been unavoidable.

THE CHAPTERS OF THE BOOK

Chapter 1 provides a brief introduction to suicide and suicide bereavement. Chapter 2 addresses the significance that taboos and stigma associated with suicide have had for the bereaved. Many want to understand their own and others' difficulties and reactions to suicide and this is illustrated through the testimonies of bereaved people in Chapter 3, while common reactions to suicide are illuminated through research findings in Chapter 4. In Chapter 5 we discuss whether it is possible to understand suicide, and we describe some of the special features that distinguish suicide from other forms of sudden death. Chapter 6 contains a discussion of common reactions in children and young people after a suicide, the factors that influence these reactions, and how adults can support children and young people affected by suicide. Because an important motivation for writing the book has been to provide knowledge and support towards coping on the road ahead after a suicide, this is discussed in Chapters 7–10: Chapter 7 is about the experiences of what those bereaved can do personally, while Chapters 8 and 9 address support from social networks and from other bereaved people; in Chapter 10 we describe the kinds of help that different groups of professionals can contribute, both immediately after a suicide and over time. In Chapter 11, using theories about grief and crisis, we show how the loss can lead to long-term personal growth and development. We conclude the book with some different ways of explaining suicide in Chapter 12.

CHAPTER 1

Suicide and the Bereaved

Life seldom deals us a harder blow than when one of our loved ones dies by suicide. The closer we were to the deceased, the greater the shock, despair and grief over the loss will be. The most dramatic situation is when children and young people lose a parent, when parents lose a child or when someone loses a spouse, cohabitant or sibling. But most of us have close ties with many people: family, friends, colleagues, neighbours or others. When the ties with any of them are suddenly torn asunder by a suicide, it almost always leads to profound grief and pain on the part of the bereaved.

Some bereaved people will, however, also potentially have feelings of relief, in the event that the deceased had been fighting a serious mental illness for many years or struggling enormously with existential problems, or because the deceased and his or her loved ones had been living with profound and apparently irresolvable conflicts for a long time. We must accept this sense of relief that the deceased will be spared further suffering or finally find peace from destructive conflicts.

SUICIDE – SUDDEN AND UNEXPECTED DEATH

Suicide always occurs suddenly and as a rule unexpectedly, even when there have been warnings of the possibility of death by way of plans or previous suicide attempts.

Even when we have been forewarned of the risk of suicide, we seldom manage to fully imagine that a death by suicide can be waiting right around the corner. And this is as it should be. We must construct our daily lives based on the belief that the all-vital life force will triumph, even for those who are struggling with serious mental health problems. In the most profound sense, suicide also challenges the very basis of our existence – namely, life itself. It is suddenly revealed to us just how thin the membrane separating life and death can actually be.

After a suicide, some bereaved individuals recognize that there were warning signs of the risk of suicide that they failed to interpret correctly. This causes many to feel guilty about not having understood the gravity of the situation and therefore not having done or said something that could have prevented the suicide. This experience of having betrayed the person in question is a particularly heavy burden for many to bear. But the experience after a suicide of having failed someone is seldom based on the actual reality of the situation before the suicide. Self-reproach often clouds the reality that one actually did as much as one could, often more, in order to support and provide help in the best possible manner. Such self-reproach causes many people bereaved by suicide to feel vulnerable. For others it can be extremely taxing to shoulder the knowledge that one was not a good enough father or mother, spouse or lover, sibling or friend, for the person who could not take any more.

> My wife was discharged from a psychiatric hospital just before she took her own life. After months of worrying and anxiety I was completely exhausted. She was also released at this time as not being at risk of suicide. I therefore believed that the danger had passed and finally relaxed in hopes of regaining some energy.
>
> Of course, I blame the hospital for not having performed a thorough enough assessment of the risk of suicide and for not having informed me of the risk factors after her discharge. In spite of this, my self-reproach has been the heaviest over the fact that I nonetheless did not understand that she was still in the realm of death's door and that I did not take better care. Knowing that it was the hospital that put me in this situation has unfortunately not helped me particularly. They have in fact afterwards simply turned their back on the discharge and the suicide.

We do not know enough of what is going on in another person's mind to be able to understand at all times the nuances of the behaviour of others and to imagine the unimaginable. The fact that very many people have suicidal thoughts in the course of their lives without putting these thoughts into action, or that very many suicide attempts do not end in death, also illustrates how difficult it can be to understand the true signs of the risk of suicide. It is in fact the case that many suicides are the first suicidal act in a person's life. In such cases, it has been virtually impossible for the bereaved to predict the suicide.

Sudden death is always a shocking experience for those left behind. This holds true for suicide, accidents or sudden death due to illness. The person with whom you were planning to share your future, for better or worse, is suddenly gone for ever, along with the majority of the things that wove your lives together.

When the future collapses, much of the present moment does as well, essentially because the present always derives nourishment from expectations about that which is to come. The bereaved can therefore experience that the only thing they have left after the suicide is the past. But even the past can appear impoverished if it is difficult to move along the emotional paths that were created together with the deceased, at a time when almost everything seems to be completely different. Memories that were full of light and warmth can suddenly become dark and sorrowful. Painful memories about conflicts can also overshadow the good memories. For many people, this is a large additional source of strain after a suicide as opposed to sudden death by accident or illness.

SUICIDE IS DIFFERENT FROM OTHER TYPES OF SUDDEN DEATH

Suicide is usually a heavier burden to bear and more difficult to handle than sudden death by other causes, because the cause of death was initiated by the deceased personally, unlike accidents, where death occurs due to something external to the deceased and was neither desired nor controlled by a personal act of will, or as a result of illness, where death crept up from within. The fact that a death has been caused by the deceased's own hand leads most bereaved people to search for answers to questions about why the deceased took his or her own life – answers that they can live with and take with them into the future.

Most people who have been bereaved by suicide find that it is important to find answers to such questions. It is important for the process of reconciliation, which is necessary in order to uphold the meaning of existence. Quite naturally, this often takes a long time. There is usually a lot to be processed, exactly because there is frequently a multitude of interwoven factors behind the suicide.

Those who have been bereaved by suicide can receive help from family or friends in their search for answers, but, for many, professional help can also be important, because it is difficult to gain insight into what was taking place in the mind of the deceased before the suicide. Precisely because suicide can be extremely difficult to understand, it is important that the process leading up to an explanation one can live with is allowed to take its own course for the bereaved. It is not always a matter of finding all the correct or final answers but rather about processing the loss and recovering meaning and mastery in the new situation that the suicide has created. For those in the daily environment of the bereaved, this can be difficult to understand.

The bereaved will not surmount grief, guilt and loss if they put a lid on their reactions. It is probably better to give oneself time to address questions in depth in order to process one's own reactions. For the bereaved, it is important to go through any difficulties or conflicts they may have had with the deceased, particularly if these have been considerable and long-term. It can be difficult to come to terms with what has happened if one does not receive help in talking about the most important aspects of the relationship, both the good parts and those that are painful. This frequently requires contact with a professional. It is, however, a condition that the professional helper has the requisite empathy and knowledge about suicidal behaviour, and not as in the following case of a chief physician at a psychiatric hospital during the third brief conversation with a father who had lost his son: 'I am tired of hearing you talk about why he died. You are never going to find the answer to that anyway. So you are just going to have to stop doing it!'

It is also important, however, that the bereaved do not end up going around in circles, brooding about the same things over and over again. Then one will dig oneself down into an inner darkness where all paths seem to lead into the past. Eventually the bereaved must move away from the deceased (still keeping them in their hearts) and into their own lives. This is made difficult by the fact that many bereaved people feel as if they are betraying the deceased by moving on with their lives.

GRIEF

Suicide is often accompanied by so-called 'complicated grief'. The grief can entail many processes and has different faces. Some feel anger towards the person who took his or her own life; some feel anger towards themselves or others they feel are in some way responsible for what has happened. Others experience first and foremost sadness or emptiness. A sense of guilt and shame is a widespread reaction. In many cases, everything is mixed together in a confusing obscurity.

It is not unusual to feel victimized by what has occurred. In a certain sense, a bereaved person who was close to the deceased is always a victim in the case of suicide, in that one is affected by an incredibly painful and extreme event. It can thus be easier to fall into the role of a victim rather than more constructive roles. As a victim, one experiences having been subjected to the consequences of something outside of the self, even though at the same time one can also feel guilty or implicated. Often the experience of being responsible alternates with the feeling of being a victim. Usually it is the interaction between people that leads to conflict and despair, without any clear allocation of responsibility or guilt. In the grieving process, the bereaved will pass through several roles in relation to the deceased, but it is important not to remain in the role of the victim, because this will make the work of taking responsibility for one's own life in the future more difficult.

Children react differently to adults. They grieve 'a little at a time' because they cannot maintain emotional intensity over long periods of time in the same way that adults can. It can therefore seem as if they are suddenly no longer grieving, immediately after having been extremely sad. It is important to support children in terms of there being no need for them to be sad all the time, but instead allow them to experience joy in the midst of all the grief. We must give them time to absorb the loss and give them permission to grieve in their own way and at their own pace, with support from caregivers. In this way they will also manage to move on with their lives.

SUICIDE IS OFTEN A CONCEALED DEATH

Suicide is in many ways a hidden death and is seldom mentioned in the media, in contrast to, for example, traffic accidents, even though in Norway each year, for example, more than twice as many die from suicide as from traffic accidents. There is also little public debate about the prevention of suicide. But while most people want greater openness about suicide as a phenomenon, we do not want the same kind of media coverage as that dedicated to accidents. To prevent the contagion effect of suicide, often referred to as 'copycat' suicides, it is essential to avoid sensational media coverage about individual suicides. Such media coverage can contribute to undermining the will to live of others on the brink of giving up, thereby leading to more suicides.

Also, out of consideration for the bereaved, media coverage of individual suicides is not advisable. But a complete lack of publicity serves in many ways to cover up suicide and could further prevent the destigmatization process that has been started in most Western societies. When accidents, large or small, are discussed in the media, this often has the effect of mobilizing local resources in support of the next of kin, a benefit which those bereaved by suicide often miss out on. Therefore, it is important that some of those bereaved by suicide step forward and provide information for the media to contribute to mobilizing help and support without letting the media dig into their 'personal story'.

THE ROAD AHEAD AFTER SUICIDE

We are all different and therefore experience serious stress and strain in different ways. We have different ways of coping with strain and different kinds of strength for withstanding it. Social resources and networks also vary a great deal from individual to individual. All of these factors imply that there are many paths 'leading back to life' for the bereaved. All advice, support and help must of necessity be adapted to this diversity, whether the latter is coming from professional helpers, other people bereaved by suicide, or the bereaved individual's own network. Because the road ahead after a suicide will always be individual and personal, it is important to be sensitive to what feels right and necessary in different situations. Inspiration and stimulation can always be taken from others, but it is the individual who is to move on with his or her life. The individual must therefore, in the final analysis, reclaim control of his or her own life.

For some, however, everything appears dark and hopeless. Particularly for those who have previously struggled with significant mental health problems, the suicide of someone close can be an additional source of strain requiring intensified mental health follow-up.

We believe that openness is extremely important for those bereaved by suicide — openness about the fact that the death was by suicide. Such openness makes it possible to verbalize what has happened, and thereby involve others on a candid and truthful basis. Openness does not, however, require the disclosure of all of the details or full exposure of all feelings. Again, it is the bereaved personally who must be permitted to regulate both the depth and form. Openness must also include clear and sincere signals of how one is feeling to the community from which one is seeking support.

When the bereaved are not open, what has occurred can be hidden, which can feasibly extend and complicate the grieving process. By not being open about a suicide, one also risks shutting out people who could have been a source of help, comfort and support, essentially because communication can become difficult. At the same time, it is important to be aware that many people have also been able to move on with their lives without having to address in any particular depth what has happened and why it happened. The path to a good future life is individual and wholly personal for every single bereaved person.

The road to a meaningful life is established first and foremost together with family and other close networks. In addition, all those bereaved by suicide should be guaranteed an offer of outreach support from professionals immediately following the suicide. Some can have a need for further professional help in the long term.

In a number of countries there are support groups for the bereaved. Many bereaved people feel that they have received a good form of help from such groups, but the benefits are dependent upon what one brings to the group personally, and there will of course be subjects that one does not want to discuss in a large group setting. Nonetheless, participation in such groups will not necessarily protect the bereaved from the development of troublesome symptoms.

Life, of necessity, goes on, for those bereaved by suicide. From experience we know that eventually life often becomes a good life as well.

CHAPTER 2

Suicide Around the World

The majority of those who lose somebody close to them by suicide are surprised about how many people there are who share their fate. Because knowledge can contribute in a positive fashion to the process of coming to terms with such a loss, this chapter addresses some aspects about what we understand by the term 'suicide' and the types of attitudes that are often connected to it. We also want to provide factual information about the frequency of suicide in different parts of the world and how suicide is distributed across age and gender. Finally, we address who is considered bereaved by suicide and how many make up this group.

Suicide is often defined in different ways, which can make it difficult to gain clarity about why people take their own lives. A definition that lies behind much of the philosophy of this book, and which is gradually being implemented in Norway and most of the Western world comes from the American psychologist E. Shneidman.[1] In 1985 he defined suicide as follows:

> Currently in the Western world, suicide is a conscious act of self-induced annihilation, best understood as a multidimensional malaise in a needful individual who defines an issue for which the suicide is perceived as the best solution. (p.203)

Here suicide is described as a self-afflicted action leading to death; it is related to many causal connections, such as the individual's vulnerability, and the suicide must be understood in relation to the culture in which the person lives. There is usually a complicated interaction between internal and external factors lying behind a suicide, rather than a single cause. In this sense, suicide can be understood as a means of finding the way out of a situation of crisis that there and then seems irresolvable for the person who takes his or her own life.

Many find it difficult to use the word 'suicide'. The bereaved often prefer other words to describe the event, such as 'to end one's life' or 'to take one's own life'. In this book we will use the different phrases as appropriate in the text.

THE SCOPE OF SUICIDE
According to the World Health Organization (WHO):

- Every year almost one million people die from suicide; a 'global' mortality rate of 16 per 100,000, or one death every 40 seconds.

- In the last 45 years suicide rates have increased by 60 per cent worldwide.

- Suicide is among the three leading causes of death among those aged 15–44 years in some countries, and the second leading cause of death in the 10–24 years age group; these figures do not include suicide attempts, which are up to 20 times more frequent than completed suicides.

- Suicide worldwide is estimated to represent 1.8 per cent of the total global burden of disease in 1998, and 2.4 per cent in countries with market and former socialist economies in 2020.

- Although traditionally suicide rates have been highest among the male elderly, rates among young people have been increasing to such an extent that they are now the group at highest risk in a third of countries, in both developed and developing countries (www. who.int/mental_health/prevention/suicide/suicideprevent/en/).

This book originates from Norway and features the testimonies of many bereaved by suicide in Norway. The suicide rate in Norway is at the middle of the international scale, so it is useful to consider recent suicide figures from Norway.

In Norway, with a population of 4.9 million, the number of suicides registered annually is relatively stable at around 525. This implies an average incidence of 11.2 deaths per 100,000 people for the past five years (2005–2009). The most recent official statistics show that 573 suicides were registered in Norway in 2009 – 416 men and 157 women. This implies an average rate of 13.5 per 100,000. It is common that about 2–3 times as many men as women die by suicide. Few young people under the age of 15 take their own lives and relatively few between the ages of 15 and 19, but from the age of 20 the rate is considerably higher. If one looks at the last five-year period (2005–2009) in Norway, men have a relatively high suicide rate from the age of 20 and for all age groups older than this. Women have a lower and relatively even curve from the age of 20, with an increase in the suicide rate at midlife and a somewhat reduced rate from the age of 60. In the Nordic region, the suicide rate is quite comparable, with the exception of Finland which is considerably higher than the other Nordic countries (e.g., the suicide rate in 2007 was 18.9 deaths per 100,000 people).

According to figures from WHO (www.euro.who.int/en/where-we-work/member-states/belarus) the rates of registered suicides vary from levels over 30 per 100,000 in countries including Belarus, South Korea and Lithuania; levels between 20 and 30 per 100,000 in countries including Kazakhstan, Japan, Russia, Sri Lanka and Hungary; levels between 10 and 20 per 100,000 in countries including Latvia, Slovenia, Finland, Belgium, Switzerland, France, Austria, South Africa, Hong Kong, Poland, New Zealand, Sweden, Canada, Norway, United States, Denmark, India, Australia and Chile. Countries with suicide rates below 10 per 100,000 include Germany, Netherlands, Argentina, Thailand, People's Republic of China, United Kingdom, Spain, Israel, Italy, Brazil, Turkey, Greece, Kuwait and Syria. In all countries, with the exception of China, the suicide rate is higher for males than for females. In rural areas in China, the suicide rate is higher among females than among males.

There is always uncertainty about national suicide statistics because different countries have different ways of registering suicide. The degree of stigma attached to suicide in the individual country will also influence how systematically suicide is registered. Nonetheless, we have a basis from which to maintain that there are great cultural differences in the scope of suicide around the world and that these are related to, among other things, psychological and social factors such as alcohol abuse and level of social integration and regulation.[2] On an annual basis, however, several million people will be directly affected by the suicide of a loved one.

WHO ARE THE BEREAVED?

Every year many people are faced with the loss of somebody close to them, among these many children and young people. We don't know exactly how many people are affected in each country – and this is of course dependent upon how broadly one defines the bereaved and their close relations in a given country.

Formerly it was thought that those who were most strongly affected by a suicide were those in the immediate family. Although as a rule this still holds true today, the reality has greater nuances in that one now includes other people who have been strongly affected by this type of death. Those bereaved by suicide can therefore include children, spouse, siblings, grandparents, all step-relations, best friends, lovers, fellow patients, therapists, colleagues – in other words, people close to the deceased who personally experience having had a close tie to them. Such a broad definition is recognized to an increasing degree within suicidology and is an important reminder of the number of people who need support after a suicide.[3]

It is therefore difficult to stipulate the number of bereaved but if one (conservatively) calculates a minimum of ten close friends and/or relatives per suicide, we will on a global basis have close to ten million newly bereaved people each year. These will be in addition to the many who have lost someone by suicide in previous years. In the course of the last ten years, we must therefore assume that approximately 100 million more people experienced the suicide of somebody close.

The bereaved come from all age groups, represent both genders and come from all levels of society and all parts of any country. When it is a matter of young people who have taken their lives, the bereaved will frequently be a spouse, young children, parents and siblings. Other relatives, friends, colleagues, neighbours, as well as the public health and emergency services, may also feel strongly affected.

A suicide is thus not something that only concerns the closest affected relations, but in fact impacts on the lives of many people.

MANY BEREAVED STRUGGLE

Research shows that suicide is an extremely stressful event for the closest bereaved, even long after the suicide. The number of people who will have exceptional difficulties will vary and some bereaved are impacted with far greater intensity and over a longer time period than others. In subsequent chapters we will address different factors that influence how the individual bereaved, family or group experience a suicide. Here we will just look at the significance that different attitudes towards suicide can have.[4]

ATTITUDES TOWARD SUICIDE

How the church, courts, politicians, public health services and other professionals working within the field of suicide define suicide is affected by and affects society's view of suicide: what the causes of suicide are and how society is to relate to the act. The way in which suicide is understood and explained in a society also contributes to creating and upholding the attitudes that the bereaved have toward themselves and how they are received by others. As such, the views of the individual on both suicide and bereavement are intricately connected with the views of society. Unfortunately, prejudice about and the stigmatization of suicide has dominated many societies.

Fortunately, attitudes change with time and there are now clear signs of change in the direction of greater understanding and less condemnation in many countries. Throughout history, the views of suicide have alternated between condemnation and acceptance. This was the case for both the person carrying out the act and the next of kin of the deceased. In the course of the last century, and in particular during the last ten years, great changes have occurred in Western culture so that a more humane and empathetic view of suicide has emerged. This has also led to changes in attitudes towards the bereaved. A historical retrospective will illuminate this further.

The Bible mentions a number of suicides without any implication of condemnation.[5] The serious stigmatization of suicide in the West can be dated back to St Augustine of Hippo (354–430) and later to St Thomas Aquinas (1225–1274). Suicide was viewed as a mortal sin because the person who took his or her own life through such an act appropriated God's power over life and death. As a result, the subject became laden with taboos and people who had been close to the deceased were stigmatized and punished. The condemnation was substantiated by important social institutions (the church and the courts) and had great significance for the bereaved for a number of centuries. In spite of the fact that important writers such as William Shakespeare and John Donne and humanists such as Robert Burton championed more understanding in relation to suicide in the 16th and 17th centuries, condemnation was predominant.

With the philosophy of Rousseau and later Durkheim's sociological observations about suicide,[6] the sin was transferred from the human being to society. This attitude also became established in society by way of legislation. Suicide was, for example, punishable by law in the sense that inheritances from those who had taken their own life could be confiscated and the deceased by suicide were buried outside of the walls of the cemetery. All such regulations were abolished in Norway through the Criminal Act of 1842. In general, the legislation in different countries has been influenced by different cultures' views of suicide, and in particular various religious communities have had an influence on legislation. For example, in the UK both suicide and suicide attempts were defined as crimes until the law was amended in 1961 with the Suicide Act. Ireland was the last country in Europe to abolish punishment for suicide attempts in 1993. No religion has a more condemnatory view of suicide than Islam. Countries with an Islamic culture have, on the whole, a much lower suicide rate than countries in the

Christian world. Other religions are to varying degrees more accepting of suicide and every country's legislation will be influenced by different religious and cultural attitudes.

Although suicide in many countries is today considered to be a socially created problem to a greater extent than was the case previously, stigma, feelings of guilt and shame are salient problems for many of those bereaved by suicide. Condemnatory and discriminatory attitudes from the legislative decrees of the past live on to varying degrees and in different ways in both individuals and social groups.[7]

BREAKING DOWN STIGMATIZATION

During the past 10–15 years a great deal has happened to contribute to breaking down the former negative stigmatization of those bereaved by suicide. A general development towards greater tolerance and more flexible attitudes in society as a whole have occurred. Not least the bereaved themselves, together with professionals, have contributed a great deal towards putting suicide and the situation of the bereaved on the agenda.

When a former Norwegian prime minister, who was also later appointed Director General of the World Health Organization, publicly stated in 1992 that her son had taken his own life, important signals were sent that suicide can happen to everyone, even those with the greatest personal resources. This has contributed to diminishing the shame and guilt of next of kin beyond Norwegian borders and contributed to greater openness and less condemnation in relation to suicide.

Other prominent individuals have stepped forward and told the Norwegian people of their own psychological ailments. This is another taboo-ridden area. Those bereaved by suicide have benefited greatly from the openness of such people. Through the establishment of survivor/ bereavement organizations around the world, the bereaved have received greater opportunities for openness and visibility (see www.med.uio.no/ ipsy/ssff/english/resources.html).

The fact that the bereaved in many countries experience less stigmatization now than just a few years ago is evidenced by how they are received by politicians, the public health services, at school, in church, at the workplace and by the general population. Politicians and public health authorities are now aware of bereavement organizations in many places in the world, which has contributed to the bereaved being seen and 'normalized' and their needs being put on the agenda by the public authorities. To an increasing extent, the bereaved speak out about what has happened at the workplace, where employers are starting to implement procedures for taking care of the bereaved and establishing colleague support systems. The same is taking place in the school system, where pupils are often taken care of through rituals after the suicide of parents or siblings. Churches arrange bereavement groups, as well as memorial services, and in this way demonstrate that the church does not stigmatize suicide and the bereaved as in former times. Likewise, clergymen and funeral directors encourage openness in relation to suicide when they meet with the bereaved.

A bereaved person who experiences a suicide today does not usually feel the need to conceal the cause of death from those closest to them, but instead is met with understanding, empathy and a non-judgemental response from friends, family and colleagues.

This is the case in many countries, but in others there are still strong taboos connected to suicide. In many countries, the taboos related to suicide and the myth that suicide only occurs in families under stress have fortunately lost a lot of their force, but they have not fully disappeared.[8]

DO SOME TABOOS REMAIN?

Although not documented by research, stories of the bereaved provide grounds to believe that some people still experience others judging them in relation to suicide. This is particularly the case for particular groups in Norwegian society and elsewhere, often defined by age, religion or ethnicity. One can experience some of the attitudes that have been abandoned by ethnic Norwegian and secularized Christians in some non-ethnic Norwegian communities or in conservative religious circles (religions subgroups that tend to interpret the Bible most conservatively). Hand in hand with the condemnation of suicide, one often finds condemnation of the bereaved by suicide. The reason for this can be that these groups have not been affected by anti-stigmatization attitudes to the same degree as the rest of the population. Because they have grown up with prejudices against suicide, the bereaved can also feel stigmatized even if those around them do not intentionally express such attitudes. Because one expects to be looked down upon, the bereaved can interpret those around them incorrectly. Stigmatization appears to occur more frequently among older people than with young people. Young people are naturally influenced by more recent attitudes. We must therefore let young people with proactive and anti-stigmatization attitudes to suicide lead the way in showing us the road ahead.

CHAPTER 3

After the Suicide

In this chapter, people bereaved by suicide tell of their reactions to different situations during the initial period after a suicide. Their stories cover only a small selection of the many situations that arise and some people have contributed several testimonials. Nonetheless, many will recognize themselves in the different descriptions. The descriptions are personal and honest and may be painful to read, precisely because the reader may identify with the contents.

THE NEWS OF A SUICIDE

The news of death arrives by way of many messengers. Usually it is brought by the police or, in Norway, by a member of the clergy. Many bereaved people react to such messengers with apparent rationality and do not properly absorb what has happened before the messengers have departed. A man who lost his wife describes his experience of the unreal situation:

> Three people were standing outside when I opened the door, two men and a woman. They introduced themselves as the police. One was a police clergyman. Inside, in the living room, they explained what they believed had happened and where. There were no witnesses and a lot of identification work remained because my wife had been injured beyond recognition. But they had found identification papers nearby which made them quite certain that it was her.
> I understood everything they said, but it was as if I was listening from somewhere far away inside my head. Their faces and voices were close up and far away at the same time. I answered their questions calmly. I went and got her hairbrush and gave them the name of our dentist, for use in the final identification. When they left, I collapsed crying into a chair. I felt infinitely alone and abandoned.

Sometimes the news of death comes before a body has even been found, because there are many signs that a suicide has taken place. How one manages to survive the hours or days until the confirmation arrives is described by this young woman who lost her mother:

They are out searching for her. The Red Cross, friends, family, neighbours and colleagues. I can't, I can't manage to go and search for my own mother. I have no strength and feel completely powerless. I look out of the window and watch what is going on. It feels as if I am standing beside myself. I am incapable of comprehending what has happened or of taking it in. I need an answer. I must have an answer.

IDENTIFICATION

It is extremely important for the bereaved to have the identity of the deceased correctly established. But the identification can both take time and be painful and difficult. A young woman who lost her mother speaks about this:

> The police need someone to identify her. It is most likely that she has been lying in the lake for two days and she looks like it. My father volunteers to do it, he does not want to subject us, his children, to the strain. I am of course relieved that he is going to do it; he wants to spare me and my brothers. But at the same time I want to spare him, I do not wish upon him the experience of going through something that may well follow him in his thoughts and dreams for the rest of his life. But we must know for certain that it is her. The person who found her knew her when she was young but was unable to establish with 100 per cent certainty that it was her, since she had suffered many injuries and a long time had passed since he had seen her last.
>
> Father leaves. It will be a few hours before this is out of the way, so we must wait even more. The waiting period is the worst, the uncertainty and not having anything definite to hang on to. After what seems like an eternity, my father calls and confirms that it is her. He was able to establish for sure that it was her. We have to trust him, even though I would have liked to have seen it with my own eyes. In order to be fully certain that she is dead – that my mother is dead.

How the final confirmation can take place is described by this man who lost his wife:

> A man from the police calls. He informs us that he is the family's contact in the case. He further explains that a final identification of my wife has been made using the dental records. There is no longer any doubt as to whether it is her. He also tells us that an autopsy has been done on her. In response to my question, he answers that the autopsy unfortunately does not explain what has happened. Nothing out of the ordinary was found and she had not been under the influence of alcohol, medication or anything else.

THE FIRST ENCOUNTER WITH THE PUBLIC ASSISTANCE SCHEME

The bereaved encounter a variety of different professional helpers after a suicide. As a rule, the majority encounter the police, clergy and doctors. In addition, many people bereaved by suicide encounter helpers from health care services (such as through a crisis team), or they come into contact with professionals from specialist health care services (outpatient mental health clinics and hospitals). In the UK, for example, the bereaved may come into contact with a coroner, who inquires into violent or unnatural deaths or deaths of an unknown cause (for more information on coroners and inquests see www.direct.gov.uk/en/Governmentcitizensandrights/ Death/WhatToDoAfterADeath/DG_006713). The experiences from such encounters are abundant and extremely varied. Some speak of good experiences from their initial encounter with the public assistance scheme, which come to have great significance for them over time. Others encounter imprudence, helplessness and insufficient knowledge, an experience that is remembered and causes pain for many years. A father who lost his son tells his story:

> My son was brought in with serious injuries to the intensive care unit of a large Oslo hospital by emergency air ambulance. I arrived accompanied by a friend shortly thereafter. We were told that he was in intensive care and we were shown into a large waiting room full of activity, a news-stand, many people, etc. We remained standing by the entrance waiting for further information. Eventually more family members arrived while we were waiting. After a while a doctor came and told us optimistically that the lungs had not been injured. This gave us hope, until a group of people dressed in white came to us and told us that there was no hope. He was in a coma and would die as soon as his heart stopped beating, something which could happen quickly or perhaps only after a few days had passed. They communicated this information to us in the middle of a huge, busy and noisy waiting room, while other people who were waiting buzzed around us. It was not until later that we were led into a separate, isolated waiting room.

In Norway, and in many other countries as well, the police force is one of a number of agencies that have taken the psychosocial care of crisis-stricken individuals seriously, among other ways by including the subject in their education curriculum. This is reflected by the fact that the bereaved often praise them for their conduct, such as this mother who lost her son:

> What was very positive about the conduct of the police was that they showed so much respect. They did not come in and take over...even

though they actually did, but they had such great respect for us and the fact that it was a private residence that they were entering. You notice such things and it means a great deal afterwards.

In some places the helpers in the first and second line services collaborate and provide extremely important psychosocial assistance for the bereaved. A father who lost his young son speaks of his positive encounter with the hospital and local crisis team:

> Our boy took his life when we were away. Our daughter found him and the police contacted us by telephone. When we arrived at the hospital, the crisis team had already been set up. They knew that we were coming. We received a fantastic reception. To use the word fantastic...but we met professionals. A psychiatric nurse, a hospital clergyman, plus, if there should be a need, doctors. Our first thoughts were for our two children who remained. We felt that we had to get home as soon as possible to help them. We had been told that it was our daughter who had found her brother. The crisis team was in this case fully aware of its responsibility. They said: 'No, you stay here at the hospital. Nobody goes home; we have already made arrangements so the children are on their way to the hospital. You will all be united here and we will try to bring in the grandparents as well.' We were given an incredible reception there. And when they came in with our son, everything was taken care of and we were able to see him. The crisis team accompanied us at all times and that was great. When night fell and my daughter and I could not sleep, we called the crisis team at 5.30 a.m. on Sunday morning. They had said that we could call at any time. Two of them came to the house on Sunday and helped out both here and down at grandmother's.

But not all professionals working in the public assistance scheme have the requisite expertise to meet the bereaved in a good way, not even in the specialist health service. A man who lost his wife tells his story about this:

> My wife had just been discharged from a psychiatric clinic. This was the only place I could think of calling when I received word. There I was put through to the physician on duty. It was late in the afternoon. Agitated, I explained what had happened. The doctor said that she would pass this information on the next day to the head of treatment and that somebody there would call me. She did not ask me if I needed anything or anyone. After she hung up, I continued walking back and forth restlessly in the recreation room, surrounded by an increasingly greater darkness.

After a short conversation at the clinic the next day, I heard nothing from them again. Nothing was organized. They did not even ring me to ask how I was doing.

A man who lost his son speaks of a lack of empathy and understanding for his situation after the suicide, also within a psychiatric institution:

My son died at a hospital from injuries incurred on the same day. I was admitted to the hospital emergency psychiatric unit that afternoon. I sank into a chair there in the corridor and sat alone for several hours, interrupted only by a nurse who came by when she was about to go off duty. 'Are you sitting here crying?' she asked, patting me on the arm, and then she continued down the corridor.

THE MEMORIAL SERVICE

Many people bereaved by suicide take part in memorials and wakes. In order for this to be a good experience, it is necessary that professionals make the necessary arrangements to ensure that the memorial will be dignified and adequate. Clergy, police, funeral directors, mental health services and others often do a good job here. A mother who lost her son tells of how many positive forces contributed to the best possible experience for her surviving youngest son:

The clergyman organized the memorial service for the young people at the boys' primary school. He had brought along somebody from the children and adolescents' mental health outpatient clinic who was to be the youngest boy's support contact. The clergyman brought him here so that my boy and the representative from the psychological/psychiatric help for children and adolescents could become acquainted before going to the memorial service. At the memorial service the young people were divided into groups with an adult and an expert in each group. The adults gathered information regarding whether any of the young people might be in need of special help. That in itself was fantastic! Everyone received clear notice in advance that no adults were to attend. The memorial service was to be the young people's. The young people had brought along photographs and candles. They managed to put it together so quickly, it was unbelievable. This took place 2–3 days after the death.

THE WAKE

Many people wish to see the deceased before the funeral. Depending upon the situation, this is arranged with the funeral director or hospital.

Sometimes the body of the deceased is so badly injured that the strain of seeing him or her will be too painful. In such a case, the body can be covered, either fully or partially, in the coffin or hospital bed. In this way, one avoids having the final memory being that of a disfigured face or body. A young man's final meeting with his mother illustrates that this can also be a positive experience:

> My mother was completely destroyed when she died. She was then brought to the hospital for an autopsy. My father and I said our goodbyes to her in the chapel there. She was covered with a thin, white cloth in the open casket. Although I could only discern an outline of what remained of her, images flickered through my mind of what the cloth concealed. But little by little it was the outline of her body itself which became predominant and the painful images became more obscure. I noticed how I grew calmer and kissed my mother one final time on the cloth over her forehead, before my father and I left the chapel together.

THE AUTOPSY REPORT

Suicide is by law an unnatural death, which must, according to official procedure, be reported by doctors to the police as soon as possible. The police determine whether an autopsy is to be performed on the deceased. This practice may vary from country to country with respect to how routinely this occurs. When an autopsy has been done, the autopsy report is sent from the hospital to the police. When the final report is submitted, the bereaved must decide how much they want to know. The police can inform the bereaved of the contents, or they can read the report themselves. If possible, someone else should be present in such situations. A doctor can also provide assistance in explaining the medical terminology of the autopsy report. Professionals have become increasingly adept at taking care of the bereaved in this type of situation, as in this case where a young man lost his mother:

> Father and I were greeted by a solemn policeman at the police station. He brought us into an interview room. There he went through the key points in the autopsy report. He took his time and was careful about not giving us more detailed information than we requested. At the same time, he gave us good answers to the things we wanted to know more about.

THE FUNERAL

Usually the funeral and the preparations for it cannot be postponed. It is important for most people that the funeral is a dignified farewell to the deceased. Many feel that it is good to have practical tasks to carry out in the midst of their despair, while at the same time these often represent a powerful encounter with new realities. A man who lost his wife speaks of how practical tasks also became for him the beginning of the grieving process:

> We have a family burial plot so we were spared having to decide where she should be buried. But we had to choose a funeral home, coffin, clergyman, chapel, date and time, and many other things. We had to decide on a ceremony, music and songs, and organize a location to gather after the ceremony and refreshments. It helped in particular to speak with the clergyman. But every decision we made felt like another goodbye to her.

Very many bereaved people tell of positive experiences in relation to their first encounter with a funeral director, and first and foremost empathetic conduct is stressed. A mother who lost her son relates:

> The people at the funeral home conducted themselves beautifully. They took time with us and spoke with us, told us what was going to happen. But I don't remember whether they told us where they took our boy. They addressed everything with my husband; I was indisposed. They sat at the kitchen table and talked.

ALL THE PRACTICAL ARRANGEMENTS

In addition to the funeral and the wake, the bereaved must attend to many other practical matters after a suicide, and such obligations must be addressed in the midst of their shock and despair. Some things can be easily put off while others must be handled immediately. Many of the practical tasks have emotional implications for the future. It is therefore particularly important that these things are done 'right' or resolved in a manner that will make it possible to live in peace with the knowledge that one did the best one could. Some tasks can involve further farewells with the deceased, such as the deletion of mobile phone numbers on one's own mobile or the closing of bank accounts. For many, these things are great challenges, also because one must perhaps do things one has never done before, or contact individuals who one has never heard of or had a close relation to. A young woman tells of how, as the eldest child, she had to take responsibility for the estate and all the arrangements after her mother took her own life. She tells here how demanding this was, both emotionally and in terms of time:

Where does one start? Is there someone who should be notified? What do I need to take into consideration and which public offices are to be contacted? I feel a bit lost, afraid of forgetting something. My mind is not exactly working in high gear; it is like molasses up there. I start by making a list. My father says that the district court is to be notified of her death, so I start there. They need a death certificate, but who writes that, actually? And what does it contain? I have feelings of inadequacy, and the road seems infinitely long. And with a head that is running in low gear, this is all the more difficult to begin with. I must after all try to come to terms with the idea that my mother is in fact dead, and that she is not going to walk in the door all confused and soaking wet. All hope is now gone. I must close this chapter and move a bit forward.

I start by calling in sick. I cannot possibly manage to organize the funeral, do all the paperwork, contact everyone who is to be contacted and complete the sale of my childhood home and many other things. My head is spinning, and I am the one who usually works in a structured manner and I don't permit myself to get stressed even if I have a lot to do. The list of tasks that I started is empty. I need an overview – a list where I can cross items off one by one. I need someone who has been through this before and who can tell me everything that I have to do, so I don't forget anything. The solution becomes the internet. I search for information there and find a lot of what I was looking for. Lists of everything from the organization of a funeral to who is to be contacted and notified. That helps me a lot. I am thus spared having to figure it all out myself; I believe that it would have been virtually impossible without having been through something similar previously.

I set myself up in the kitchen. Have my PC sent here from home and buy a printer, folders and other office supplies. Create an office and start organizing all the papers that are floating around. Bills, letters, appointments, pay slips…

Some people bereaved by suicide dedicate a lot of time to and address their grief by putting a personal touch on the final farewell, such as through a type of monument. A father tells of how he had decided to find the gravestone for his young son as a final gesture that he could make for him:

Oh God, how we looked and looked in search of the stone. Sunday after Sunday we went and dragged ourselves from place to place. We walked and walked. We were never satisfied. But finally we found the stone. Although the funeral home advised me not to engrave the name ourselves because the craftsmanship would not be good enough, I did it myself. I received a lot of praise for the stone as well as for the work of laying it. I think that such things have an incredible significance. It is part of your processing, participating and speaking about it. That is what I think is the most important.

The significance of taking the time to help out in taking care of practical matters is expressed by this man who lost his wife:

I still haven't deleted the mobile number on my mobile phone or deleted her files on the PC. But I have saved both in such a way that I do not see them on a daily basis. I am thinking about waiting to delete them until it feels right to do so. For the time being, it feels right to have saved both. It is like saving things that are still important, even though on a daily basis they are hidden from me.

My sister went through her clothing for me. I couldn't bear to address her questions when there was something she wondered about. It was an enormous help for me that she did this. Most of it went to the Salvation Army. But every garment was like a new and painful farewell.

CHAPTER 4

Common Grief and Crisis Reactions

NORMAL REACTIONS TO AN EXTREME EVENT

For most bereaved people, suicide occurs like a bolt of lightning out of a clear blue sky. Sudden and unexpected death, often in a life phase when it is not common to die, usually produces grief and trauma reactions in the bereaved that have a number of common characteristics. First and foremost, one experiences the feeling of a complete lack of control. But it is extremely common that those bereaved by suicide also experience feelings of guilt and ponder unanswered questions. This is so central to the entire grieving process after a suicide that it is discussed here in a separate chapter (see Chapter 5).

A common denominator for strong reactions to suicide is that they are normal reactions to an extreme event. But it is also normal that some do not experience the reactions that are discussed below to any notable extent. Recent research findings[1] show that around one-fifth of people bereaved by suicide do not experience strong or multiple reactions, either a short time after the event or later on. Grief is private and personal and will therefore always be unique for each bereaved individual.

EARLY CRISIS REACTIONS

The reactions arise in the initial hours, days, weeks and up to the first months following a suicide. These are normal reactions, which for most will diminish with time. The strength of the reactions and how soon they make themselves felt also varies greatly. And for some the reactions can continue for several years.

Unreality

This description was given by a young woman who lost her mother:

> I feel as if I am standing outside of myself looking in. I look at my family and the police officers who are in our living room. It is an absurd situation. Time stands still and it feels as if the entire world has come to a halt and everyone in the world knows what is going on in our living room right now. Outside a powerful storm is raging and the wind takes hold of the corners of the house so the walls creak. The light in the living room is an artificial yellow and seems virtually unreal. I have a feeling of being a part of a bad reality programme on television where my family is this year's selected contestants. I hold my breath. I think that I will wait to breathe when everything has passed on its own. I wait for the pain to subside and for everything to go back to the way it was. Two days ago, my life was completely normal; now it has been turned upside down. The focus has been moved. My head is full and empty at the same time. There is no space for anything more there, while at the same time it is essentially empty and I must invest all of my energy in just staying upright. I go into a kind of state of flux in which everything seems endless. I have no idea how I am going to move on, or where I will go or turn around. I catch myself thinking a thought which I have never thought before: I no longer have a mother. My mother has chosen to reject life; she did not want to be with me any longer. I must manage on my own now, be a big girl, a good girl. I just have to find a way to get out of this state of flux first. Manage to understand that this is about my life and that I have the leading role in the reality programme this time.

When somebody suddenly dies, most bereaved people will experience a sense of unreality when they learn of the death or during the waiting period before receiving clarification of what has happened. This can be experienced as if everything seems to be taking place in a dream, as if it is happening on film, or as if it is not true. There is the sense of standing outside of oneself and being a spectator and it is difficult to absorb that one is really experiencing what is taking place. A mother describes how for months she was obsessed by the idea that her daughter had not taken her life after all. The thoughts returned again and again:

> I tried to analyze whether I had forgotten some piece or another along the way, so that she was here somewhere after all. I had just lost her for a while. It was a bizarre business. My brain just did not understand it.

Time stands still

The experience of time can be dramatically altered, often with a feeling that time stands still so that the grieving person can blame themselves for not having reacted quickly enough. The waiting period before help finally arrives can seem endless, allowing time for many thoughts. If the death takes place in the home, the bereaved will often act adequately and quickly until others step in and assume responsibility. They summon help, start resuscitation attempts if they think this serves a purpose, and as a rule act wisely, quickly and constructively. Previous experiences, such as from a first aid course, are retrieved from the experiential layers of the brain, and information from the surroundings is taken in quickly, clearly and in detail. All of this combined provides a solid starting point for handling the situation.

The experience of unreality is a reflection of the fact that the emotions are put on hold, which serves as a protection from pain. All of the person's energy can thus be used to address the situation that has arisen. Nevertheless a number of bereaved people will blame themselves afterwards for the way they reacted. Many think that they did not react adequately. Others can regret that they did not have a chance to say farewell at the moment of death because they were busy with desperate resuscitation attempts, which they later understand had been futile.

The shock

Most people experience severe shock reactions when they lose a loved one by suicide. One feels numb, dizzy and completely overwhelmed. One can feel as if one is outside of one's own body, and experience confusion and a sense of the unreal to such a great extent that one feels completely numb. Many have difficulties speaking, thinking clearly or focusing. Bodily reactions such as shaking, heart palpitations, nausea, chills or dizziness are not unusual. For some, these reactions continue after the first day and are intensified by a lack of appetite, too much coffee on an empty stomach and so on. Many bereaved people speak of an avalanche of different thoughts cascading through their minds: 'What now?' 'How will this go?' There are so many things to address at the same time and everything seems chaotic and confusing. While some people have exceptional memories and remember details from the hours and days after the suicide, others scarcely remember anything at all from this period.

Most of those who experience such dramatic events have never before experienced anything similar. It is not unusual for some to become extremely frightened and wonder if they are personally going to die from the shock, as was the case for this woman who lost her daughter:

> When I got off the bus, he wanted us to sit down on a bench. Then he said: 'Jane is dead.' Just like that. It was like an explosion. I thought it was strange that I did not die, actually. I could have died, because there was an insane explosion in my head. I thought: 'Am I dying now? What is happening?'

The initial shock reaction provides an immediate type of emotional protection. The altered experience of time provides 'extra' time for processing and permits the affected individuals to take in what has happened, little by little. Strong reactions are simultaneously postponed so that the bereaved is not immediately overwhelmed by feelings leading to paralysis that will render them incapable of action.

The shock is so strong that essentially one is not capable of taking in everything that has happened all at once. For that reason, hours, days, weeks or much more time can pass before the bereaved person fully realizes what has happened. One 'knows' with one's thoughts but not with one's feelings. The bubble that one finds oneself in contributes to enabling constructive and rational action and this can be extremely important in terms of moving on later, as for this mother who lost her son:

> I believe that I remember those initial days after Stephen died with crystal-like clarity. It was as if I were watching a dramatic movie. There were practical things to be attended to and there were relatives and friends who had to be informed. This all went very smoothly.

It is extremely important that those around the bereaved have an understanding of this initial survival mechanism, so that they do not expect the bereaved to necessarily have strong immediate reactions or put pressure on them to react in a certain way. Such reactions can explain why it is those who are closest to the deceased who must sometimes comfort those who are not as close. It is also easy to start using phrases such as 'You are taking this so well' or 'You are so strong' to describe the reactions of the bereaved and thereby put expectations on them to continue to react in this way.[2] Many who experience being protected by shock reactions during the initial days will cry later on, such as at the wake, pre-funeral devotion, memorial service or funeral. The rituals can help the bereaved to understand and take in what has happened.

REACTIONS OVER TIME

While the immediate reactions often include shock, a sense of the unreal and numbness, accompanied by strong feelings, the subsequent reactions often vary in quality and over time. The post-traumatic reactions are a part of our normal pattern of reactions to profound loss and are not morbid processes.

These are reactions which in different ways help us during the period after a death (and following other situations that threaten our existence). The most common post-traumatic reactions are these:

- self-reproach and guilt (addressed in Chapter 5)

- re-experiencing or avoidance of what happened

- anxiety and vulnerability

- disturbed sleep

- lethargy and dark thoughts

- concentration and memory problems

- irritability and anger

- physical ailments

- feelings of grief, loss, longing and pain.

Re-experiencing what happened

Elements of what happened in connection with the death, such as visual or auditory impressions, can have been etched into the mind with an unusually strong intensity. The same can occur if one was not present – one develops fantasies about what may have happened or about how the death occurred. People bereaved by suicide may also have seen or heard terrible things, been exposed to unusual odours or touched extremely unpleasant things in connection with the death and these can be re-experienced as a kind of flashback. Professionals often hear that the bereaved have so-called flashbacks or intrusive sense impressions on the retina which they cannot rid themselves of. Examples of other things that can have become deeply embedded can be the telephone call communicating the death, the meeting with the clergy or police who arrived at the door with notification of the death, the period of waiting for news or the last thing one said to or did with the deceased.

It can be extremely disturbing to re-experience such memories or fantasies and they can impose themselves in such a way that the bereaved feel that they do not have any control over them. It is believed that such post-traumatic reactions are related to emotional mobilization mechanisms, where the brain must quickly take in information from the surroundings in order to orientate itself in the situation and determine what must be done. If such reactions continue over time, one should seek help from a professional with trauma expertise (see Chapter 10). In particular one should be observant of those who discover deceased family members. It can be important for them to receive adequate assistance to prevent the dramatic impressions from becoming intrusive and lasting flashbacks.

But not all bereaved people experience recurring images or memories as something negative. The bereaved can see the deceased in front of them, fully lifelike, and it is only when they reach out to touch him/her that they understand that the person is not there. Sometimes they hear the voice of the deceased or feel as if the person is in the room. Many seek proximity by smelling the clothes of the deceased, retrieving things they associate with him or her or carrying with them some object that connects them to the deceased. Some process the impressions so that they gain control over the memory images and use them in a positive manner. For some, a part of the grieving process will therefore be to keep the thoughts and images alive. A mother says:

> The image of Jack sitting on the couch, dead, is there all the time. It followed me everywhere during the first year and was disturbing. I will never be rid of it – I don't want to be rid of it either. And therefore I say that I will not call it a strain. I remember very well that I sat there and held him and he was cold and stiff. But that was the last farewell we had with him. That image remains there, it should remain there. But it is not a strain. It is something I have grown accustomed to and that is how it should be. I will not forget Jack and I don't want to be rid of the images either. They don't disturb me although sometimes it is painful.

What happens when we miss somebody with great intensity after a sudden death is that the brain builds bridges which alleviate the loss by giving the bereaved a strong experience of closeness to the deceased. This need not be something negative, but it can be if this impinges upon the ability of the person to function on a daily basis.[3]

Avoidance

For many who experience intense and invasive thoughts and images, an attempted solution can be to push these away, to avoid feelings or thoughts about the death or to refrain from speaking about their pain. For some, this is a coping strategy that they use during the initial period; for others, it can become more permanent. Some speak of how they witnessed horrible things in connection with the suicide, but they have managed effectively to repress this for many years and dread bringing it to the surface again, such as through psychotherapy. This can function well for some, but for others it can lead to constantly expending a disproportionate amount of energy on keeping the impressions at bay.

People bereaved by suicide do not only experience being invaded by impressions from the incident itself for a long time afterwards. For some, things that remind them of the person they have lost can also become difficult in daily life. A mother spoke of how a year and a half after the death she avoided emotional associations with the daughter she had lost:

> I have not been able to read poems and novels and listen to emotional music and the kind of music that Jane liked. I did so to begin with and wailed and screamed, but now I manage not to. I must keep far away from such emotional things. I am too weak. I try to control it by avoiding what mobilizes the big wave.

Anxiety and vulnerability

Anxiety and fear are also very common reactions to a sudden death. If the consciousness is full of the past, with disturbing memories and difficult thoughts in connection with what has occurred, the present can come under pressure from both the past and future. The anxiety can be more random or it can be connected to a specific fear that something else will happen to one's own family or oneself. When the intensity of the latter reaches a high level, it is called catastrophic anxiety.

Catastrophic thinking entails that one expects further catastrophes: 'Because one death has happened, another one will certainly occur!' The world is experienced as unsafe. The sense of security and invulnerability that many experience in daily life, and which enables us to hold the suffering of others at a distance, is replaced by a new vulnerability where anything can happen. The suicide leads to a generally higher level of preparedness involving anxiety about new catastrophes. Parents can, for example, become more vigilant and protective of surviving children. The fear that something will happen to them can be unbearable. This frequently leads to over-protectiveness. Because the child's fear of losing his or her parents also increases after a death in the family, the foundation for vicious cycles is established. This can have an impact on people bereaved by suicide for decades, although the acutest feeling of catastrophe is most intense during the first years. Several years after her son took his own life, a mother relates:

> For a long time I found that I was compelled to check on the children after they had fallen asleep. I was prepared to encounter a catastrophe whenever I opened the door to their bedrooms. I remember my pulse, my breathing and the knot in my stomach when I opened the bedroom door as paralyzing. At times, the same feeling of catastrophe can still descend upon me; it passes more quickly now, but it is a feeling of paralysis. In a way, the body is set at catastrophe preparedness. There can also be sounds or smells that provoke the feeling of a catastrophe.

Anxiety can also have other dimensions. One is an increased sensitivity to change that many experience. The body is set at emergency preparedness, and all changes in the surroundings, from sudden noises to sudden movements, are interpreted as dangers that trigger a reaction. Many of those bereaved by suicide have their insecurity reinforced by reading the newspaper, particularly obituaries, and by watching the news with new and vigilant eyes, and have the sense that so much more happens now than before. Many people around them do not help matters when they tell the bereaved of their own or others' losses, often because they believe that this will be helpful. Instead, it can reinforce the experience the bereaved is having that 'so much happens'. Many bereaved can therefore be disturbed by an indeterminate anxiety, as described here by a young woman who lost her mother by suicide:

> I go down to the bathroom again, concentrate on remembering all the way down so as not to repeat the wasted trip of earlier. There is a strange atmosphere down there. It feels as if I'm not alone. A cold gust of air greets me when I go around the corner at the bottom of the stairs. In the hallway leading to the bathroom it is terribly cold, a breeze. A door bangs. A cold chill runs down my back, I shiver – hurry into the bathroom, do what I need to down there and run up again. There is something in the basement that is not right. I hear noises down there all the time even though I know that there is nobody there. There is a negative tension throughout the entire house. As if there is something in the air, infecting it.

It is extremely exhausting, in terms of both emotional and physical energy, if on a daily basis one goes around worrying and in a state of vigilance in preparation for what could happen. One gets tired, but not in a way that results in a good night's sleep.

Disturbed sleep

Often thoughts about what happened arise after going to bed and many acquire sleep disorders to a greater or lesser degree. Most struggle to fall asleep because their thoughts cause agitation in the body. Some fall asleep easily enough, but awaken early in the morning, without any chance of falling asleep again. Sometimes what happened returns in the form of a nightmare. If one has to get up early to go to work or is responsible for getting the children off to school, the night becomes extremely short. Anyone wishing to show their willingness to be involved and offer support should wait to make contact until the late morning, so that the bereaved can have the chance to sleep. Those bereaved by suicide who have serious sleep disorders will naturally not be able to be fully productive, either at school or in a work context. We have witnessed that when the quality of sleep is diminished over a long period of time, this can easily have the effect of further compounding other post-traumatic reactions.

Lethargy and dark thoughts

Many bereaved people describe lethargy as a reaction to suicide. Grief requires an enormous amount of energy. Beyond this, the combination of disturbed sleep, confusing thoughts and a poor appetite will for many result in feeling physically and psychologically exhausted. They can feel constantly tired and lethargic for a long time after the death. A father who lost his son says the following about this:

> It is about the same as if a valve is opened below so that all of the energy in the body drains away. You have no energy for anything. You sit in the kitchen from half past five wide awake, but there is no compulsion in the body to go to work. It is empty. No energy… It is frightening how tired the body is. Constantly tired, as if one had run 20 kilometres.

For some, the strain of a suicide can also lead to depressive emotional responses and extremely dark thoughts. Some think that they could just as well have died personally, like this mother who lost her son:

> The entire second year was brutal; everything was black and just became more and more black. The pain grew more and more intense and throughout the autumn I had only one thought in my head and that was that I was responsible for Scott's death. I had failed in my job of being a mother. I had clear perceptions about the fact that I should die instead of continue living. In my darkest moments I saw myself as a murderer.

In connection with the depressive emotional response, as mentioned above, many experience sleep disorders and in particular early awakening. But many also have an extremely unnatural need for sleep and can sleep away large portions of the day. One experiences constant sadness and despondency that does not appear to become easier, either through positive events or attempts at encouragement and support. Further, one often experiences a reduced desire for and interest in things one was previously interested in and a reduced ability to enjoy the company of close family members and friends. It can be difficult to get started on daily activities, and everything goes slowly. Concentration and memory become noticeably worse and suicidal thoughts and attempts can occur. Thoughts about it being 'my fault', 'I am just a burden' and the like are common. Some bereaved also gain weight from comfort eating, while others lose weight because they are unable to eat enough. Although most bereaved will experience one or more of these reactions for periods of varying duration, the reactions will not automatically qualify them for a diagnosis of depression. If such a pattern is maintained over time, a physician will potentially assess this as depression, for which the bereaved should receive treatment.

A depressive emotional response can, like anxiety, be the result of the experience of having lost control and feelings of helplessness and inadequacy. A strong sense of guilt, combined with the painful experience of loss, reduced energy and strength, can increase the risk of such reactions. Information and understanding that getting through traumatic experiences is a drain on physical and emotional energy can have a preventive effect. Due to the physical and emotional strain that the situation following a suicide entails, a number of bereaved people take sick leave from their jobs. Although this can be necessary, at the same time one should be aware that sickness absenteeism can lead to increased social isolation. If one can manage it, continuing in one's job – possibly with a reduced schedule – can help to prevent a depressive emotional response.

Concentration and memory problems

Grief often causes concentration and memory problems. Many people bereaved by suicide have believed that they were in the process of going mad, or that their ability to think had been permanently impaired. They speak of how they organize their life by writing messages to themselves on Post-its so as not to forget daily errands.

The cause of such thought-related difficulties is uncertain, but it is probably associated with the fact that intrusive memories and thoughts are a source of constant disturbance and interruption. In particular, individuals who saw the deceased at the moment of death, or who found the deceased either dead or badly injured, can struggle with tasks requiring concentration. A reduction in the speed of thought processes, as a result of sadness and attempts to keep the uncomfortable memories at a distance, can also be a contributing factor. Regardless of the cause, many report impaired short-term memory and problems in focusing their thoughts on tasks requiring complicated cognitive activity.

Some people can, over time, have such pronounced concentration difficulties that they can feel as if they are physically but not emotionally present. This can be experienced as extremely uncomfortable and frightening, as this father who lost his son relates:

> I remember that we sat here and were going to watch a film. Afterwards we were going to talk about what we had seen. Nobody remembered what they had seen. We had laughed and everything, but to this day nobody remembers what we saw. And then I grew frightened. That in that situation I was physically present and saw it, but I can't remember names or...

Because such problems can persist for a long time, they can create difficulties and worries for those bereaved by suicide in a school or work situation; difficulties in making decisions and in getting work done and an increase in errors can occur. Colleagues and supervisors who do not understand this connection can become irritated when they discover that tasks are forgotten, take longer to carry out or are not completed with the same quality as previously. For the bereaved who experience such reactions, it is important that the work situation is adapted to their temporarily reduced work capacity, so that they do not wear themselves out trying to manage everything (see Chapter 8).

Irritability and anger

Irritability, impatience and anger are also common reactions. This may be due to some of the factors mentioned above: lack of energy, poor sleep patterns and so on. But it is also the case that heightened sensitivity to one's surroundings and the change in values that many experience result in the bereaved imposing different requirements on their social environments and they can therefore become more easily irritated or angry. Frequently, it is anger both towards the person who took his or her own life and against oneself or others. Some also have a justifiable anger towards a health care system that they feel has let them down or caused them great additional strain.

Physical ailments

As a result of the huge psychological strain that those bereaved by suicide are subjected to, physical illness and bodily reactions are extremely common. As a result of a generally increased level of bodily arousal, one can experience muscle tensions and strong physical pains (e.g. in the chest), stomach/intestinal upset, shortness of breath, palpitations, dry mouth and headaches. Many chronic conditions of pain can be related to unprocessed grief. A loss of appetite can lead to a deficiency in vitamins and minerals that the body needs. Over time, one can become more predisposed to different types of illness because the immune system does not function as it should. Bereaved people often point out the connection between a suicide and family members' increased physical ailments afterwards, such as a young woman who lost her brother:

> All the colds I had! I think that the immune system... I think you can have a number of illnesses that are so-called latent. When something like this happens, then you have no extra resistance. Then I think it happens very quickly. When I look at my father and everything that happened afterwards. And it is clear that when you are grieving, you become even more afraid if you contract some illness or other, right? You don't need that in the midst of all this.

GRIEF

'There is no stronger expression of love than grief.' This quotation is our starting point when we speak here about grief and grief reactions. Grief is not an illness, but it can sometimes lead to illness. Grief reactions following a suicide vary in intensity and duration and find expression in many different ways (see Chapter 11). While some who have been bereaved by suicide have only subdued reactions, the reactions of most are extremely strong. Bereaved individuals who have extremely strong reactions sometimes wonder whether their reactions are 'normal', or if they are in the process of going 'mad with grief'. Many have a great need for confirmation that what they are experiencing is 'normal'. They are relieved when they learn that their reactions are viewed as normal reactions to an extreme event.

Feelings of loss, longing and pain

The majority of the bereaved cry and experience intense sorrow and longing for the deceased. The strong sense of loss, longing and pain arise, as a rule, with the greatest intensity after the funeral, with the resumption of daily life. The loss of the deceased can then be omnipresent. It is both a physical absence, such as no longer being able to hold a child, embrace a loved one or share life together with a spouse, and, not least, the absence of all of the activities which wove one's life together with that of the deceased, which greets the bereaved in everything they do. For very many, the period from three to twelve months after the death is the most difficult period. At all times one is surrounded by memories of the deceased, and all holidays and anniversaries (the deceased's birthday, the anniversary of the death) are experienced for the first time without the deceased. The daily sense of loss and intense longing is often intolerable, while at the same time one can feel lonely because there is nobody else who can fully understand one's grief experience.

Those bereaved by suicide also speak of how before the death they thought about grief and pain as synonymous. After the suicide, they experience that the pain must be described separately, that it is a purely physical pain, 'like an amputation without anaesthesia'. A father choking back sobs points to his heart when he speaks about some of the most painful things following his son's suicide: 'It's a pain located here. The physical pain of it, I would not have believed it. Because it is physically painful.'

Grief over time

For most, the grief and feelings of loss change over time, although for many these feelings never go away. Most do not wish to forget. After a year, the tears can still be there, but they can change in character. The body will return more to normality, but the feelings of loss can be strong, as with this mother:

> During the initial period it was as if I had a stone as heavy as lead in my stomach. It was also a physical sensation. Like a nauseating and heavy burden. After a while, the burden became lighter, and finally disappeared. I can't remember exactly when the feeling disappeared, probably around the same time as when I started in treatment. I can still sometimes feel the knot in my stomach, but it does not have the same force as before. My crying has also changed. First it was just deep and hollow. Then there were periods when I just had the need to shout/roar like a wounded animal. Now when I cry it is different, it is crying over that which will never be, the type of loss that comes from a lost future.

Grief reactions over time will also relate to how the bereaved are treated by the people around them. One of the worst things for many people in mourning is when self-proclaimed experts lecture the bereaved on their knowledge of grief. Their intention is to offer comfort, but they succeed only in creating frustration and withdrawal on the part of the grief-stricken individual with their 'good advice'. A typical statement might be 'Once the first year has passed, you'll see how everything gets much better. Then you can begin to look ahead and put all the sadness behind you.' Unfortunately, the bereaved receive such advice from both professionals and their social networks. As we will explain later on in this book, grief does not follow a streamlined pattern; it varies for each individual and is related to, among other things, the individual's state of mind on any given day, the time and the place (see Chapters 8 and 11). The myth that grief ends after a year has long since been disproved. On the other hand, for most people, though not everyone, the nature of one's grief does change so that it becomes easier to live with, though it does not necessarily disappear.

Complicated grief reactions

It is when grief reactions continue over time and create barriers to leading a normal life that they must be viewed as complicated and unhelpful. There are, however, several types of complicated grief reactions. If one suffers for months an intense and persistent longing for the deceased, difficulties moving on in life and an experience that life and the future are without meaning or purpose, this can be a sign of complicated grief. This is also referred to as 'extended grief' or 'chronic grief'. It is the separation from the deceased that is at the centre of one's existence and which finds expression through persistent crying, longing and preoccupation with thoughts about the deceased. To a certain extent, this entails difficulties in understanding and accepting that the death has taken place. Grief may also be complicated when it is postponed, in the sense that the expression of grief may be delayed or avoided.

We speak about complicated grief only when the experiences are uncommonly intense, prevent functioning in daily life and have continued for at least six months. Complicated grief reactions that are caused by separation from the deceased should also be distinguished from depression and anxiety-related conditions. The bereaved are not, as some fear, in the process of 'going crazy'. Recent research findings show that those bereaved by sudden deaths such as suicide, murder, accidents and unexpected infant death are at greater risk of developing complicated grief than with other types of death. Research has also shown that people with complicated grief are at greater risk of persistent health problems.[4] It can therefore be important to receive the help of a psychologist or other qualified helpers with such conditions.

For bereaved individuals who are struggling with complicated grief reactions, good social network support is extremely important but not always sufficient. There are effective therapeutic treatment methods that help those who are struggling to process their loss, by identifying and changing difficult thoughts and interpretations of the death (see Chapter 10).

Grieving differently or out of sync

It is easier for me to talk about it outside the home. If I need to cry for a while, then I do, but he doesn't. He puts on a kind of mask that says that everything is fine. When I am depressed and crying, then I get angry with him. For then I feel that he should also cry. But then he says: I am grieving, too. I am longing, too, and I am in just as much pain as you are but I don't cry.

The above quotation illustrates a typical example of how women and men can grieve differently and how this can cause an atmosphere of mutual reproach between people who are grieving and who are very close in daily life. There can be considerable gender differences with respect to grief, an issue which is beginning to receive increasing attention. Women react usually with greater intensity and for a longer duration than men, although in around one-fourth of cases the opposite is true. One often sees that while men actively relate to and take action in relation to the external world by way of organizing the funeral, making arrangements with the police and funeral director, women can be more predisposed to introspection, in addition to experiencing and expressing strong emotions. In general, women tend to seek out others to talk about what has happened to a greater extent than men, while men will seek to concentrate their thoughts on other things, or they work to avoid strong feelings or to distract themselves. We can view this difference as 'looking inward' versus 'looking outward'. It is important to note that this does not necessarily mean that women grieve more than men, but rather that they frequently express grief in a direct way. The difference in the manner of grieving can lead to mutual reproaches on the part of both men and women, and communication and reciprocal support can become difficult, as was the case for this woman who lost her daughter:

My husband says that sometimes he is able to distract himself when he is working. I stay home and look at the photographs and am in the midst of all the memories. But he is in a lot of pain inside. I am not in so much pain because I am more outgoing. I cry more and am able to talk about it more.

In couples or among several family members, 'grieving out of sync' can also occur. For some, it is difficult to burden family members with their bad days, because one wants to spare the others, who appear to be having an easier time. This is also the case for children and young people (see Chapter 6). In other families, one manages to take advantage of the benefits of grieving out of sync. Here family members manage to regulate this in the form of a helpful interaction, in which some show their grief while others provide support. Because not all family members are feeling down at the same time, they can also take turns pulling each other up. A father who lost his son describes how the fact that he and his wife were up or down at different times became a source of strength:

> In the beginning it was as if when Susan was up I was down and vice versa. We gave one another balance. When things were really crazy and I was at rock bottom, she would be able to say, 'Let's go for a walk now, now let's do this or now let's do that.' That continued for two years.

Because grief can be such a huge, heavy burden, there will be periods when one will not manage to be a resource for other family members. It is thus important to have knowledge about different grief reactions. Such knowledge can contribute to increased understanding and less reproach in relation to those who are reacting differently.

CHAPTER 5

The Unique Aspects of Reactions to Suicide

Other forms of sudden death cause many similar experiences and reactions on the part of the bereaved. Nonetheless, there is something about suicide that makes it a distinctive type of death. In this chapter, we discuss why and how suicide can be a particularly heavy strain for bereaved individuals who were close to the deceased.

DEATH THAT IS SELF-INFLICTED AND A REJECTION

The fact that the death has been self-inflicted distinguishes suicide from other types of sudden death and leads, for many, to extensive speculation about why it happened.

> I struggle with thoughts about what happened every single hour and I struggle with it every single day. I have a theory, but is it correct? Why did it happen? And how could it happen? That is the part that is a heavy burden to bear.

As was the case with this father two years after having lost his teenage son, many bereaved people struggle to reach an understanding for several years after a suicide. Particularly when young, apparently well-functioning human beings take their own lives without their closest family having picked up on signs or verbal cues about what was about to happen, it can be extremely difficult to understand that death became 'the solution'. All factors are examined critically, from childhood to the present, including illnesses and events leading up to the suicide.

The majority of bereaved people have a need for answers and explanations for a suicide. Even though the grief and loss is not diminished by an explanation of why a spouse, father, mother, child, sibling or lover took his or her life, many bereaved people experience that they are then spared the additional burden of speculating about the motives of the deceased. The need for an explanation of the death is expressed by a father who lost his 20-year-old son:

Had there been a letter in which Henry had written: I had predilections that I couldn't manage to live with, I knew this about homosexuality and parents and did not want to disappoint you, etc.... Then you could have looked at the concrete cause of Henry being unable to continue. But when there is nothing... Or it would have been so much simpler had I received a report from the Driver and Vehicle Licensing Agency stating that the right tyre exploded and it rammed into a rock-face, that that was the cause. The grief and loss would have been the same, but you would have something concrete when you stood beside the tombstone. It happened. Now we have nothing.

From time to time, questions arise about the connection between intention and action. Did the deceased understand the ramifications of the act of suicide? The question is particularly relevant when children take their own lives. Then one might ask: Was the death the result of an accident while playing? Or was it a desire not to live any longer — and, if so, did the child understand that death is final? Professionals also ask themselves such questions. With or without help from professionals, many bereaved people find answers or theories that they can manage to live with. Others manage to accept that they will never receive a final answer. Many, unfortunately, continue going round in circles over their questions for a long time.

Sometimes conflicts with and negative events in relation to the deceased can have played a part in the outcome. The bereaved can in such cases be left with thoughts about how the deceased can have felt betrayed, rejected or violated by the bereaved personally or by another closely related individual.

But the deceased can also have been the instigator of conflict and a poor problem solver, where the bereaved did not succeed in providing help. The suicide can then be experienced as a complete rejection on the part of the deceased. Interpersonal relationships are seldom purely good or purely bad. For those bereaved by suicide, it will facilitate the process of coming to terms with the death and the grieving process to establish a balanced image of what characterized the deceased individual's relationship to them. Professional help will be needed to achieve this.

STIGMATIZATION, SIN AND SHAME

Shame and stigmatization are experienced differently in different cultures.[1] In some cultures, those bereaved by suicide can feel that they are different, excluded or second rate, depending upon the prevalent attitudes to suicide in the individual society (see Chapter 2).

The stigmatization finds expression in many ways, such as at the funeral and other mourning rituals being passed over without the possibility for others (outside the closest family) to attend. Many bereaved people first learn about other suicides after they have informed those in their surroundings of the suicide in their own family. A mother described this after her son's suicide: 'One learns about other suicides when one experiences it personally, because then one is exposed, standing there completely stripped down. Then others are able to come to you and speak of their loss.'

Those bereaved by suicide relate that they are often uncertain about what is being said about them and about how others perceive the fact that the deceased took his or her own life. In a study of young people bereaved by suicide, it was found that they felt that they were different or stigmatized because the death had been self-inflicted.[2] They expressed feelings of shame and the experience of being a 'leper' in social gatherings with others, something which contributed to many attempting to hide what had happened from people around them. Although attitudes similar to this certainly linger today, in Norway, for example, there are a number of indications that young people in particular do not view suicide with the same judgemental eyes as many older people. But some still live with strong religious convictions that suicide is a sin. A mother who lost her son overheard her own parents telling her adolescent daughter that it is 'a serious sin to take one's own life. You brother will not go to heaven'. The woman had these reflections about this:

> My parents are very old and for them there is shame associated with taking one's own life. My mother believes accordingly that one is thereby not allowed into heaven. It is a serious sin to take one's own life... My mother certainly thought that this would have a preventive effect on our daughter; she wanted perhaps to prevent her from doing the same thing as her brother. Instead, it was horrible assertion to communicate to a grandchild.

Although in Norway there are few people bereaved by suicide who directly express that they feel shame after a suicide, there appears to be an element of shame in statements such as 'if only he had just been run over' or 'if only it had been an accident'. People's reactions in relation to the bereaved by suicide can also reinforce this underlying shame, as with this woman who lost her son:

> The whole shame business is something that I have registered. I have to admit it. Is there really somebody who thinks that I must feel ashamed? Because that was how it was before. When people turn around on the

street and stare it can serve as a confirmation and it can make you extremely sad and it becomes even more of a strain if it is like that.

When people who take their own lives have an affiliation with groups in society that others look down upon, this can lead to double stigmatization. The bereaved can then feel further degraded and devalued even though the people around them do not directly express such attitudes. A father of a young man who took his own life and who was also a drug addict experienced a strong feeling of being 'second-rate':

> That we would have a son who would take his own life – it has been hell, to put it mildly. One encounters a sense of failure. Had it been an accident, illness...but exactly the fact that he took his own life, then there are all the questions. Yes, we are left with the feeling of being second-rate. In addition to this he was just a drug addict; he was just one of the others.

In the course of recent decades, knowledge and increased openness about suicide and the situation of the bereaved have contributed to breaking down some of these prejudices. It is to be hoped that more knowledge about the complex factors behind suicide will contribute to further diminishing prejudices.

Suicide will often be interpreted as a meaningless and 'final' solution to experiences of difficulties for which the deceased there and then must have found to have been without a solution. For most people, these problems could feasibly have been solved if the deceased had experienced any hope of recovery, of a lessening of existential pain or of being able to find a way out of an extremely desperate life situation.[3] Many of those bereaved by suicide dwell on thoughts that they could and should have intervened or helped out by providing contact with necessary assistance – if they had only known the extent of the problems the deceased was struggling with. In a suicidal process, it is not always possible to help and it hurts many people bereaved by suicide to think about how much pain the deceased must have been in during the final period, without their having been able to help out.

FAREWELL NOTE

Regardless of what may have taken place before the suicide, some try to make it easier for those whom they leave behind by writing a goodbye letter in which they absolve the bereaved of responsibility and guilt. But some suicide notes contain strong accusations. Research shows that 25–50 per cent of those who take their own life write farewell notes or letters. Some write in depth to explain why they are taking their own life. Reasons can be financial embezzlement, long-term serious mental health problems, substance abuse problems or a generally intolerable social situation. Others write that conflicts in the family or with a lover were unbearable, or that the rejection of a loved one made life intolerable.

Some deceased send messages to their loved ones in other ways. Some send messages using more spontaneous forms of expression, such as words on a dusty car window, a text message or through symbolic objects which the deceased leaves behind. These are often more indirect messages that can be difficult to read and understand. A young woman who lost her mother relates:

> I was puttering around a bit on my own in the new apartment and found something that I think seems strange. She had collected many of my things in a drawer in the bathroom – the spoon from my christening, a scrapbook and some photographs. These are not things that one keeps in a drawer in the bathroom. And in her bedroom I found several of my things gathered together on a shelf. The hat from my graduation, a ruler with my name on it and a handbag. Otherwise there was nothing in the closets, either on the shelf in the bathroom or in the bedroom. In the storage closet, I found my doll's house from when I was a little girl, which I was sure had been thrown out a long time ago. I get a creepy feeling that she was trying to tell me something by doing this. It is as if she is sending a signal that I am supposed to live here now. It seems almost as if she has passed on the baton to me, now I am the one who must take care of the family, keep us together.

Some messages from the deceased direct reproaches or accusations at the bereaved, for example by mentioning infidelity, divorce or other relationship-related problems to those they leave behind. It is important that this is not brushed under the carpet or unilaterally rejected as unreasonable, but that the bereaved attempt to arrive at a balanced perception of the situation. For many bereaved by suicide, it can be extremely difficult to distinguish between what one personally must take responsibility for, what must be attributed to the interactions of the relationship, and, possibly, what must be attributed to the deceased. Because it is extremely seldom that there are simple explanations for a suicide, many people bereaved by suicide may benefit from speaking with professionals about how the interaction between many factors might have led to the tragic outcome.

Most experience it as good to have received a final farewell, although a farewell letter seldom makes it possible to understand fully why a person ended his or her life. If nothing else, one is able to establish that it was an act of will and not an accident. A mother explains how important the farewell letter was in terms of diminishing her feelings of guilt: 'In the beginning I read and reread his letter and knew that nobody could have stopped him. The letter was incredibly helpful in terms of keeping us from feeling guilty.'

In spite of a suicide note, most of those bereaved by suicide will nonetheless speculate about many unanswered questions for a long time after the death.

THE FINAL MEETING

Many people bereaved by suicide experience that the final meeting or the final conversation was painful and full of conflict, as is the case for this young woman who lost her mother:

> I think back to the last conversation that I had with my mother. It was approximately one month ago. I noticed it the minute I opened the door to my childhood home. The same feeling I got every time I came arose this time as well. The negative atmosphere – my spirits fell. I greet my mother, who smiles a cold smile without looking at me. I can feel how it all begins to boil over. I have had enough of this, can't stand feeling this negative atmosphere any longer.

For many bereaved people the last thing that was said or done can overshadow all previous experiences, good or bad. Perhaps the conflict of the final meeting involved factors that were connected with the person in question taking his or her own life. It is then easy to conclude that one has contributed to the suicide. And because suicide can be experienced as if somebody we love has made a choice to leave us, a final meeting full of conflict can contribute to increased feelings of guilt on the part of the bereaved. It is then particularly important to be able to keep in mind that there are always complex causes behind a suicide (see Chapter 12).

SELF-REPROACH, REPROACH AND GUILT

Self-reproach, reproach and feelings of guilt are extremely common after a suicide. 'What could I have done to prevent what happened?' and 'If only...' or 'Why us...?' are common thoughts. In contrast to death by illness or accident, where most loved ones can share responsibility with external factors, those bereaved by suicide are often burdened by a special type of guilt, mixed with feelings of responsibility, speculations about why and other reactions to the death.

A mother and father who received a farewell letter and partially understood why their son took his life, nonetheless struggled to understand the way in which he died. Their own attitudes and the attitudes of others to suicide influenced them, and shame, guilt and speculations about why became intertwined:

> Had I been aware that the death would be so difficult due to the way we lost him... I don't believe that people are aware of that. For an accident it is also painful. But there you have an answer that such things happen. But when you experience someone taking his own life, there are then so many other questions. What is wrong with us, and didn't we do enough and...

Self-reproach will frequently also be connected with feelings of reproach in relation to other family members, such as partners, ex-partners, siblings and parents. Reproach after suicide can also be directed towards outsiders, such as therapists in the mental health care system. In Norway today, for example, approximately 25 per cent of all suicides occur while the deceased is still undergoing treatment in the mental health care system or immediately after discharge. Many bereaved people find it particularly difficult that the suicide took place at a time when they were sure that the deceased was in safe hands or had been discharged after a reassuring evaluation. Along with anger about the fact that others did not take enough care, these bereaved individuals also blame themselves for not having done enough or for not having been more active in relation to the hospital or in acquiring more information.

Many people bereaved by suicide ask themselves questions such as 'What kind of mother or father have I been?', or 'What is wrong with me – didn't I do enough?' When it is a child or adolescent who takes his or her life, the self-reproach is often particularly strong. But we also find that these roles are reversed, so that children and young people can assume the blame for the suicides of parents or other family members. Researchers describe how young people are disturbed by questions about why family members wanted to depart from this life, their own contributing role in this decision and their experience of having failed to prevent the death. Some young people are obsessed by thoughts that 'if they had only done this and had not said that', then it would not have happened.[4]

It is important that the bereaved receive help in reviewing the life of the deceased in ways that can give them the strength to absorb the fact that the suicide was connected with factors that the deceased experienced as a strain and also with relational factors. In terms of the process of coming to terms with the suicide, it is important to recognize that both the deceased and the bereaved were and are ordinary human beings who have not been solely positive in relation to one another, that conflicts are a part of life and that coming to terms with such a loss entails that one also manages to address the difficult aspects. Most do the best they can, and we must live with the fact that this is not always sufficient.

A daughter's thoughts about guilt

Reflections and thoughts about guilt can alternate between what one personally experiences as irrational and rational, and one can find oneself caught up in emotional chaos, as was the case for this young woman who lost her mother:

> It is my fault. Completely and totally my fault that she could not take any more. It all became too much for her and it is my fault. My fault that I did not see that she was ill. My fault that she could not take any more. My fault that she did not receive help.
>
> I should have noticed. Her own daughter should have noticed that she was ill and helped her to get well again. I should have visited her more often, I should have talked to her more, talked about how she was feeling and kept her spirits up when she was down. I don't understand how I will ever be able to forgive myself for what I have done, or perhaps more for what I have not done. Perhaps I did not want to see. Can that be a possibility? That I saw but nonetheless did not see.
>
> She was always the strong one. The strongest person I have ever known. She was like a rock that has stood firm for thousands of years and that never falls down. Invincible. Nonetheless, she was the one who couldn't take any more. It is so incredibly difficult to understand. Difficult to understand how she was thinking and difficult to understand how she really was feeling.
>
> Those around me say that it is not my fault. That there is nothing that I could have done differently. I tilt my head a bit to the side, smile and say, 'No, no, there was nothing I could have done. I could not have prevented it.' They mean well and are trying to comfort me and make me feel better. Inside I am thinking, 'Of course I could have prevented it. Of course there was something I could have done.' They have no idea what they are talking about. They don't see that I could have done so much to help her if I had only seen that she needed me. All those times that I was irritated with her, talked to her in a way that no mother deserves, contradicted her instead of agreeing with what she said. Had I only seen – had I only known. Then I would never have contradicted her or been irritated with her. Then I would have been kind and easy-going all the time.

It's so strange that she didn't say anything to me. She didn't want to bother me with her problems. She probably wanted to spare me, protect me. She was the adult, I was her child whom she wanted to protect. I would probably have done the same thing. Would not have said to my own child that I was in pain, not physical but psychological pain. It would be frightening for a child regardless of how grown-up this child was…at the very least I understand that.

CAN GUILT HAVE A FUNCTION?

When we hear about how guilt can tear apart those bereaved by suicide, it can be difficult to imagine that it can serve any purpose. Nonetheless, guilt can have a function.

Reproach and guilt are among the most important reactions we have following extremely critical or traumatic events. When we carefully sift through everything we could have or shouldn't have done, thought or said, the brain is working on retrieving information about our experiences that we can use later in life. If we did not possess this mechanism, we would not learn from our mistakes, change our behaviour and develop as human beings. It is only when we continue with such self-reproach after all the relevant information has been retrieved that this mechanism becomes self-destructive. It is therefore important to respect that there will often be such a period of soul searching immediately following a death, that it must run its course and that it is only later that we will be able to know whether the mechanism has had a natural progression or if it has become fixated. It is important not to remain in a state of unreasonable self-reproach. If such thoughts are especially strong or persist over time, they can diminish quality of life to such an extent that the bereaved may need professional help (see Chapter 10). Those who were struggling with anxiety and depression before the suicide can be at particular risk.

To be able to come to terms with the suicide of a loved one, so that one can move on in life with one's head held high, it is important to recognize that none of us fully understands what is going on in the minds of those closest to us. Neither do we always understand the kind of impact our behaviour has on others. Even when our loved ones speak openly about their problems, we are not always able to be there for them in a good way. Being human entails making mistakes even if we have the best intentions of helping, but for most of us this means that we do the best we can. A person who has taken his or her own life has closed the door on help and shut others out. Although it is extremely painful to be excluded, it was ultimately the choice of the deceased to turn away from possibilities for help.

CHAPTER 6

Children and Young People Bereaved by Suicide

Adults worry a great deal about children who experience the suicide of loved ones. Often these adults do know how they can best provide help, but sometimes they do not have the extra energy required to do so.

FACTORS THAT INFLUENCE CHILDREN AND YOUNG PEOPLE'S REACTIONS

Much like adults, children and young people's reactions after a suicide vary greatly. Children are also dependent upon those around them to an even greater extent than adults. Their reactions are determined by age and developmental stage, how the suicide was explained to them and their understanding of death, their relationship to the deceased and whether they were present when the deceased was found. Beyond this, the child's daily life situation will also have an impact on the grieving process. This is particularly true with respect to the parents' resources and life situation, the communication climate in the family and between parents and children, previous traumatic events in the family, the support available in the family and how the child is received by friends, the school system and their social networks.

Age and developmental stage

As early as the age of two to three years, a child can begin to understand partially what death means if one of their loved ones die. They may ask where the person went, and perhaps go looking for them, such as for mother or father. At the age of five to six years, death is experienced as more irrevocable, and the child will be able to put the death into a context of external factors such as accident or illness. Nonetheless, they do not fully understand that the person in question will never come back. They can, for example, ask about who is going to bring the person food in their grave or when they are coming back. Such questions also illustrate how concrete the mentality of preschool age children is.

When a child has reached the age of eight or nine and older, they will understand that death is final and that mummy, daddy, a sibling or grandparent will never return. They understand that the body does not work when it is dead, that one cannot breathe, eat or walk. In contrast to slightly older children, eight- or nine-year-olds will not worry about whether they personally are going to die. The thought that everyone is going to die sometime and that it will also happen to them can, however, be a part of the reactions of the bereaved in early adolescence. Older children will often relate to more existential questions – both the unique aspects of a particular death and about death in general – such as thoughts about justice, the meaning of life and fatalistic thinking. While younger children are completely dependent upon information, support and explanations from their most important caregivers, in order to be able to address what has happened, support from friends, school and other social networks plays an increasingly more important role as children grow older.[1]

The relationship to the deceased

The relationship that the child had to the deceased will usually have great significance with respect to how he or she reacts to the death. Relationship here means:

1. psychological closeness (for example, the strength of the emotional tie the child had with the deceased)

2. biological closeness (family connection to the deceased – for example, a parent or sibling)

3. social role (for example, if the deceased was a father figure or sibling-type role model).

When a child or young person loses a more peripheral person, the emotional closeness they had to the deceased will have an impact on their reactions. There will potentially be large differences in the reactions to the loss of a grandmother who was a second mother compared to a grandmother whom the child only met every Christmas. There is also a greater chance of children being able to handle the death more easily if the most important caregivers have had a somewhat more peripheral relationship to the deceased.

When a parent or sibling takes his or her own life, children and young people will experience a threefold loss because the parents or remaining parent have/has such a hard time that this will have an impact on the children. They will possibly feel rejected both by the deceased mother, father or sibling and by the surviving parent. The children's loved ones can be so consumed by their own grief that the children are forgotten or do not receive the care they need. Children often think that the parents are suffering more than they are, and thus do not always dare to express what they are feeling themselves. For that reason, researchers have called these children 'the forgotten bereaved'.[2] One also sees how outsiders often give more support to siblings with the loss of a parent than with the loss of a brother or sister, in spite of the fact that parents can actually be more affected and incapacitated in terms of taking care of their other children when they lose a child than when they lose a spouse.

Losing a child by suicide is such a huge burden for a father or mother that it will always result in difficult and unstable surroundings for the surviving children. We often see that younger children who are still living at home have greater difficulties than older siblings. The explanation for this can be that the family burden for younger siblings can be greater than for older siblings, because they spend more time at home together with their parents. Older siblings who have established their own nuclear family are 'protected' by this.[3]

In addition to the grief and loss, when one of a child's parents takes his or her own life, the child loses an important role model. This can create insecurity and affect their sense of self. In addition to identity problems, many young people also find that they assume new roles in relation to surviving family members, something which in turn can influence the caring climate.

The caring climate

For children and young people, care from the most important caregivers will be crucial to how they handle a suicide. Research has shown that the degree of psychosocial problems experienced by children and young people is connected to parents' or caregivers' psychological and social difficulties. After a suicide in the family, in some cases one can see that children and young people's normal development is delayed due to a lack of emotional support from grieving and despondent parents.

When adults have lost a partner or a child, we often see that the children and young people are only partially taken care of by the family's network, because the main focus is on the parents. Although many young people maintain that the death has a stronger impact on the parents than on themselves, it is painful to experience coming second, as for this young girl who lost her brother: 'We are like, just siblings. That is what I think you feel, because your parents are really in pain, right. And you understand that, because they have lost their child. But I have lost my brother...'[4]

Although many understand that the parents are suffering and incapable of giving the children the support they need, this does not diminish the children's need for support and help from adults. The same is true when a parent loses his or her partner. Then many young people experience being left alone in their grief, because the remaining parent has more than enough in dealing with his or her own grief and shock.

Role reversal

In cases where adults have such strong reactions that for a period of time they are unable to take care of themselves, children may assume adult roles and take over as caregivers. Older siblings can take over responsibility for younger brothers and sisters, or they can temporarily take responsibility for cooking or other parts of the caregiver role that their mother used to perform before she died. It also happens that young people who have moved away will move back home to take care of the surviving parent and younger siblings. If nobody else steps in, children and young people can have significant experiences which can come to affect them over time, as for this young girl who was 16 years old when her father took his life:

> I could not have accepted support from Mummy or the family during that time, it would not have worked. Because you see that she is in such pain and you don't want to. I had to feed Mummy the first day. Nothing worked.

In addition to the fact that such role changes contribute to relational difficulties in the family, it will possibly deprive the young person of a relatively carefree childhood or adolescence if they are obliged to shoulder an adult caregiver's role at far too early a stage. If the children's closest caregivers do not have the strength or energy to take care of them, they must receive help in order to prevent them from being pushed into such roles.

Keeping secrets, silence and blocked family conversation

Because grief is affected by one's manner of thinking about the reasons for what happened, 'black holes' can also arise in the grief, whereby adults and children are unable to share all of their feelings and thoughts. In interview surveys of next of kin and loved ones, carried out long after a suicide, adults who were children when a suicide occurred express intense frustration over what they experienced as the keeping of secrets, silence and blocked family communication after the death.[5] Family secrets often arise in connection with a suicide, where some family members know and others don't. In the worst cases such secrets can affect the family for generations; it is much better if the secrets are shared before too much time has passed. Difficulties in expressing grief openly in the family after a suicide are often due to the fact that everyone is affected, a lack of emotional closeness and communication in the family before the suicide, or family members protecting one another. When family members do not manage to share their experiences and thoughts, in some cases this can lead to extended and complicated grief processing for children and young people.[6]

If children, young people and adults have very different access to information after a suicide, this can also create difficulties for the children's processing of grief. It is not unusual for family members to have different perceptions of reality with respect to how the deceased was feeling during the period before the suicide, what actually happened or why the suicide occurred. For example, the parents, on the basis of their knowledge about their child, can have difficulties understanding why their child took his or her own life, while the children in the family may have another source of information which gives them a theory about why the suicide happened. Conversely, it is conceivable that a surviving parent can have knowledge of suicidal thoughts before the death or of a serious situation that may have triggered it. In particular, it will be difficult to understand the suicide if a mother or father takes her/his life subsequent to prior conflicts and difficulties that they have concealed from the children.

An important reason why adults attempt to hide information from children and young people can be the wish to spare them from the realities. This can be a matter of an autopsy report or a suicide note that contains painful information. This information nonetheless constitutes a reality, and what has happened has happened. If adults have such information, they have the possibility of integrating the facts into their perception and way of thinking about the suicide, in a manner which the young people cannot. Children and adults may then attempt to understand what has occurred from extremely divergent points of view.

Feelings of guilt because openness about 'secrets' could perhaps have prevented the death can be extremely heavy to bear and it can be difficult to share such information with others after the fact. If different perceptions of the cause of death become the most important topic over time, adults and children can, due to accusations or feelings of guilt, be prevented from sharing their thoughts with one another. This makes mutual support difficult and can contribute to unnecessary speculations and frustration in young people. It is therefore important for the grieving process that family members have a certain common understanding of the realities surrounding the death and how this is experienced by the different members. Children and young people have different understandings of death at different ages, and this also increases the necessity of discussions and the exchange of information and of adults exploring what young people are thinking about a suicide in the family. It is also important to repeat this with time as young people develop an increased capacity for understanding.

Protection that hinders communication

Another important cause of a lack of open communication in the family is that many parents attempt to protect the children from seeing how much their mother and/or father are suffering. Along the same lines, there are many young people who undercommunicate the grief and despair they are carrying in order to protect their parents or other adults.

A number of young people withdraw from their parents in order to avoid becoming despondent themselves. Many parents also overprotect their children after a suicide in the family, because they are afraid that something bad is going to happen to them. Some children and young people can have a hard time handling being overprotected, while others understand that it 'just means that they care about me a great deal'. Other young people want to protect their parents from seeing how much pain they are in. They pull themselves together or make themselves scarce so as not to burden their parents further. This is a strain for young people, and presumably some of the descriptions of anger and a lack of self-control in other situations can be attributed to this. A 17-year-old who lost his mother said: 'I can't manage to cry in front of Daddy, I have to manage on my own. But it reaches a point where I can't take any more and then I completely fall apart.'

COMMON INDIVIDUAL REACTIONS

Research shows that young bereaved people are affected more profoundly and more in the long term by suicide than they are with other types of death. They experience intense and confusing feelings, which are often viewed as being connected to the fact that the death was self-inflicted. Their grief is also frequently more pent-up than for other types of death. In order to be able to provide the best possible help, it is also important to understand that many of these difficulties in principle are not only individual, but rather relational and social in nature. They are to a large extent dependent upon all the conditions surrounding the young person.[7]

Immediate reactions

Most young people are even less prepared for the possibility of somebody taking his or her own life than adults are. Shock, numbness and a sense of unreality, followed by vulnerability, sadness, loneliness and desperation, are common immediate reactions. Over time, young people can exhibit a lack of energy, sleep disturbances, appetite disturbances and weight problems, an increase in emotional and physical arousal, feelings of guilt, social withdrawal, concentration problems and varying degrees of problems at school, while younger children can be afraid of falling asleep out of fear of not waking up again. Some become angry, frustrated, have suicidal thoughts, depressive moods or anxiety reactions. Others develop personality changes, reduced self-esteem and an identity crisis, particularly in connection with the suicide of a close family member. Young people bereaved by suicide also experience more physical ailments than is the case in reaction to less dramatic deaths.

Some children and young people have only some of these reactions, while others may have many. Sometimes adults are surprised about the fact that children do not react more than they do. This is particularly true for children of pre-teen age, who, after they have been informed of a death, can continue playing as if nothing has happened. Young people can quickly insist on being allowed to go out with friends or to school. These types of reactions are often about self-preservation, through which the young people seek out familiar and safe surroundings in a situation in which the world has become chaotic and unsafe. Although it is held that children and young people should be given the opportunity to grieve in the period immediately after the suicide so as to diminish the risk of their struggling with reactions at a later date, normal grief reactions in children and young people vary from almost no reactions to delayed grief, grief that lasts a long time or grief that is extremely intense.[8]

Feelings of loss and sadness

Feelings of loss and sadness manifest themselves in many ways in children and young people who have lost a parent or sibling. The feelings of loss are often the worst, and for some young people this is so serious that they do not function in daily life or at school in the period following the death. They are continually reminded of the loss and longing for their mother, father or sibling when friends and classmates as a matter of course speak about their own parents or siblings. A 16-year-old describes her feelings of loss and vulnerability after the death of her mother:

> For me the fact that I can't call for Mummy is the worst part. Because that was, like, what I did the most. Regardless of whether I was afraid or whatever, like…everything. Yeah, just having a mummy, just that. There are very many such comments in my class: 'I have to call my mother,' 'Mummy is coming to pick me up', etc. You start thinking about it right away.

As is the case for adults, young people can also experience hearing the voice of the deceased or seeing him or her before them. This can be extremely frightening if the child does not know that this can be an ordinary and normal reaction. To assuage feelings of loss, many children and young people will seek out places that they associate with the deceased, spend time looking at photographs or ask adults about their memories of the deceased.

Anxiety

Like adults, children and young people can struggle with vague anxiety after a suicide. What was secure becomes insecure, and what was previously comprehensible appears incomprehensible. Younger children can fear that others in the family or they themselves are going to die and they can seek out security by becoming more clingy. They can become afraid of being away from their parents, want to sleep in the same bed or refuse to stay at home on their own. It is not unusual for young people to develop more general catastrophic thinking that something is going to happen to other people they care about. A 17-year-old sibling said this:

> I understand that Mummy and Daddy are worried about me. But I am actually just as worried about them…often. Many young people don't tell their parents that they are scared to death that something terrible is going to happen again, because they feel that their parents have more than enough just dealing with themselves.

Anger and guilt

Frustration, anger and instability are extremely widespread in children and young people when they have had a close relationship to somebody who has taken his or her own life. Both girls and boys speak of how they have become more angry and stressed. Small things can appear to be extremely unfair after the death, and trivialities can trigger fits of anger and frustration. This can take its toll on younger siblings or others close to them. A young boy who lost his mother said:

> I go around with so much inside of me that if some tiny triviality comes up that disturbs me in a manner more than everyday things…it happens that everything just falls apart for me. That is no good. I feel pretty unstable at times.

Usually, the anger is directed towards the deceased, but it can also be focused towards oneself or other family members. Children and young people can be angry with caregivers, surviving parents or other adults who they perhaps feel were not attentive enough or had not done enough to prevent the suicide. Many are angry with a deceased parent, sibling, boy/girlfriend or friend for choosing death as the solution for his or her problems. For many children and young people, it is difficult to understand that the deceased could choose to leave them and the family to struggle with all of the problems. They can also be angry at parents because they meddle too much in their way of handling the death, such as by implying that the children should grieve in a different way. Others become angry because of inadequate parental support or because they experience that caregivers are more concerned about the deceased than about the bereaved. A common reaction among those who feel anger is an accompanying feeling of guilt for these feelings.

Children and young people can also feel guilty and blame themselves for the death because they did not prevent it or because they feel that they contributed to it. They often remember the last thing that was said, and if it was an argument or hurtful words, this is often a heavy burden to bear (see Chapter 5).

Depressive reactions and suicidal thoughts

Studies have shown that one-fourth of all children and young people struggle with depression and anxiety symptoms during the first year following a suicide and many can struggle with despondency for a long time.[9] Although such reactions usually recede eventually, they are more widespread in families in which caregivers or the children have struggled with mental health problems before the suicide occurred.

Researchers have held[10] that when a loved one dies, bereaved young people experience that death becomes extremely present and that the risk of suicide can therefore increase. Because a suicide changes the grieving young person's role, identity, expectations and daily tasks, it can lead to brooding about whether life is worth living. The greatest risk for such a development arises if a young person represses his or her grief.

After a suicide in the immediate family, up to one-third of young bereaved people can experience suicidal thoughts, which fortunately seldom lead to suicidal actions. One therefore assumes that the risk of suicide does not increase after a suicide unless the young person is particularly vulnerable and that vulnerability is compounded, if, for example, the caregiving environment is extremely poor. Many young people wonder about how the suicide will affect them in the future, and some are worried about whether taking one's own life can be 'genetic'.

Intrusive memories and images

Both adults and young people can struggle with post-traumatic reactions in the form of intrusive memories and images. The memories can produce physical arousal but can also lead to spending a disproportionate amount of energy on trying to avoid thinking about or addressing anything that reminds them of the death. In particular, children and young people who discover the deceased, or who have had intense experiences in connection with this, are predisposed for such arousal, avoidance or intrusive memories. These young people are also more likely to have depressive reactions, reduced energy and more physical illness and muscle tensions than those who do not experience intrusive memories and images. In such cases, the young person needs professional help.

A young girl who lost her brother by suicide illuminates the many different reactions that young people can have. The young girl experienced her brother taking his own life when she was 16 years old. She was alone at home when she found her brother in the neighbouring house. Here she speaks of her reactions a year and a half after the death:

> In the beginning, the first six months, maybe a whole year, I struggled enormously with the image of where I found him. But finally it became an image that I came to terms with. It did not hurt any more; it became an image of no consequence. But then it returned in a nightmare where I found him in other ways. I found him around where I was walking. I dreamt that he came back and then killed himself right in front of me. I am terrified of going into his apartment and still can't do it. But I dream about going in. It is horrible thinking about how cold he was and how hard he was. I can feel it all the way to my fingertips, to put it that way. Right now this business about my brother has been sort of put aside. I have perhaps repressed…I have not felt anything in particular. In the beginning I felt nothing. Then there was a period when I could start

crying. I can't now, not even when I have been drinking. It's kind of shut off. You reach a point where enough is enough. I have a need to shut it off. Then I have other types of reactions, physical reactions. I have been sick a lot, especially during the past half-year. So that is how it has surfaced...

The testimony above illustrates how intense, varied and persistent the reactions can be in young people who experience finding a person they have been close to who has taken his or her own life. The girl describes a sensation of complete unreality and numbness in the beginning. The impressions were so strong that effective defence mechanisms were mobilized. The sensation of unreality and numbness protected her from her own feelings. Gradually she started struggling with more and more common post-traumatic reactions. The sight of the place where she found her brother, the feeling of touching him and the completely unexpected situation of suddenly finding her brother disturbed her for a long time. The girl speaks of how she alternately approached and distanced herself from things that could remind her of her brother, both when she was awake and in her dreams. When she was awake, her anxiety kept her away from the place where she found her brother, while she approached it in her dreams. Because she could not, with time, stand this mental activity, she invested a lot of energy in turning it off. The result was that the painful and difficult things that she suppressed surfaced in the form of physical illness. This is also a clear example of why professional help must sometimes be brought in.

YOUNG BEREAVED PEOPLE AND THE SCHOOL

Very many children and young people who are bereaved by suicide experience great difficulties at school. They spend large portions of their daily life in school, and it is there that they meet requirements for performance and achievement. Their experience at school is a good scale by which to assess how they have been affected by a suicide.

Concentration and learning problems

Studies show that many young people develop problems with learning new material and with concentration after a suicide.[11] Although children and young people can also experience impaired concentration in their free time, it is in school that this becomes most evident and is most disturbing. Children and young people can go from being good achievers at school to developing such acute concentration problems that they are unable to keep up in class. Up to several years after a suicide, close to one-half report that they 'almost always' have difficulties concentrating. The concentration problems at school can also be related to a lack of sleep, as this 12-year-old who lost his mother points out:

> You try to sleep but it doesn't work. And even if I am going to go to school the next day, I often don't get to sleep until 2–3 a.m. and I have to get up very early, so then I only sleep for a few hours.

Typically, such concentration problems entail thoughts about what has happened arising when there is little other distraction. Assignments that are enjoyable and call for activity in dialogue with the teacher or classmates are easier to concentrate on than quiet individual work and difficult or boring assignments. The painful thoughts remove the focus of attention from what the teacher is communicating and reduce the possibility for learning or concentration on schoolwork assignments. The thoughts are especially intrusive when the class is silent or while doing reading assignments at home. Concentration problems can lead to young people failing exams or a serious decline in their marks. Many find that they need both more time and more explanations than previously to learn new and difficult things. A 14-year-old who lost her mother says the following:

> It's just like you can't even manage the multiplication tables, you know? It takes me a lot longer to understand that a calculation is the way it is. I need a much better explanation. Especially new and difficult assignments suffer because new information is not 'stored'.

A young boy who lost his big brother put it like this: 'I am very good at just listening, but I don't store it. It goes in one ear and out the other.'

A lack of understanding

Young people have an easier time keeping intrusive thoughts and memories at a distance when they do enjoyable things or are active, such as during break. Teachers who observe that children play as if they hadn't a care in the world during break and then become sad and pensive in class can easily misunderstand and believe that these children are taking advantage of the situation to get out of doing their schoolwork. Young people who do the best they can, in spite of concentration problems and headaches, can develop depressive thoughts if they feel that they are under constant pressure, in particular the pressure to get good marks. External pressure to perform and excel can further compound an intense internal pressure. Gradually, these young people can begin to feel like losers because they can no longer perform at the same level as before the suicide or in relation to what teachers, in spite of the death, expect. For some, this can hinder further schooling in that they do not receive the marks necessary for acceptance to a certain course or college. In the worst case, the child drops out of education.

Although difficulties with concentration and learning are the most common school-related difficulties, one should also be aware that some children and young people overextend themselves during the initial period after a suicide, by working so hard that they improve their marks during the first chaotic months. The school and homework assignments are then being used as a kind of escape from the painful situation and as a means of creating order amidst the chaos. For outsiders, it appears as if these children are managing very well, until they are 'punctured and go flat' after six months and their marks nosedive. But there are also some children and young people who progress through the period after the suicide quite effortlessly, including with respect to their schooling.

In spite of widespread difficulties with schooling, children are nonetheless often left alone with their problems. Better follow-up on the part of the school is therefore extremely important for young bereaved people. Although many schools today do a great many good things for these children, there is often a need for further knowledge in order to be able to provide better help. These problems highlight the need for parents to liaise with the school. In the UK special consideration is given by the examination boards following bereavement such as suicide.

RELATIONSHIP TO FRIENDS

Children and young people's social networks are extremely important after a suicide. While younger children often confide in their parents about their grief, fewer teenagers do so. They are far more inclined to open up to close friends in their own age group. It is therefore extremely important for friends and girl/boyfriends to be there for them.

Understanding in the network of friends

The most important friend is the friend to whom one can tell everything, and very many young people experience having such a friend. Girls, however, to a much greater extent speak with their girlfriends than boys do with their friends. However, the deep conversations which young girls can have can lead to these girls dwelling too much and for too long on things that are sad and painful because they have a good listener. If one starts spinning one's wheels without moving forward, the person can also become locked in grief and this contributes to increased anxiety and depressive thoughts, and to isolation from other friends.[12] The ways that boys tend to react, speaking little and with a lot of physical and other activity, therefore have a number of positive aspects. Young people are best helped in processing their reactions if they manage to utilize the positive grief-coping strategies of both boys and girls. Friends who knew the deceased are especially important for many bereaved young people, because they can share memories, grief and feelings of loss and because they are in a sense in the same boat.

The young people's difficult situation can also make them vulnerable to words and expressions of youth culture, such as 'go hang yourself', 'so shoot me' or 'so shoot yourself'. Such expressions are often used without any intention to hurt.

Alienation from friends

Most young people experience being met with empathy and consolation from their network, particularly during the period leading up to the funeral. But after a while many young people find themselves on the sidelines in relation to their group of friends. They speak about experiencing their old friends as childish, immature and interested in completely insignificant things, while they personally have gone through an abrupt maturation.

Through crisis and growth, many young people experience increased self-knowledge and personal maturity which has an impact on their relationships. This sudden maturity often implies that they grow out of their old friends. They may seek out new friends who are older than them, something which is not always a good idea. Although young people who are bereaved by suicide have matured cognitively, they may nonetheless remain behind at the emotional level. One young person spoke of how his brother's death had matured him:

> You feel as if he has, like, gone into you, so that your age is twice what it was. Now I no longer spend time with kids my age, because they are so immature, but instead spend time with people who are a lot older than me.

An 18-year-old who had lost his father relates:

> I turned 35 a bit too quickly, I think. I acquired a completely different view of things compared to friends of the same age. I took things a lot more seriously, something which I did not always find to be much fun. You have a completely different type of life after something like this.

> There is no doubt that I saw the gravity of things in a manner that was completely different. Things were damn meaningless at times.

Much like bereaved adults, young people speak of a new era, a new scale of values, life outlook or even a new identity in the aftermath of the suicide of a loved one. While the death results in increased self-knowledge and personal maturity (see Chapter 11), the changes are extremely demanding because they cause huge upheavals in daily life. Many in the same age group do not understand that grief takes time. Friends implicitly express that they are growing tired of hearing about the suicide, or that over time it becomes too much of a burden to relate to it. Friends can therefore pull away from the bereaved or vice versa. A young boy who lost his brother says the following about this:

> I feel that friends say it, without saying it, that now enough time has passed, that it's enough. The old friends, those who have known me the longest, are actually the ones who back out. It becomes too much for them and they can't cope with it personally.

Due to what they have experienced, many children and young people no longer manage to amuse themselves and behave in a carefree manner like others of their age, or they have adult thoughts which other young people are unable to relate to. Young people can afterwards feel as if they missed out on a part of their childhood, because they were not emotionally present. They can experience having lost important months or years of their lives. Some don't manage to take part in high school graduation celebrations or refrain from going to parties which they would have otherwise attended, and when they are ready to take part, they find that they have missed the boat.

HELP FOR CHILDREN AND YOUNG PEOPLE

Children and young people have the best conditions for coping with a suicide when they are living with resourceful parents in a good family situation, when the communicative climate is good and there is mutual support within the family. For various reasons, not all of these conditions exist for everyone.

The extent of closeness in the relationships between parents and children and young people after a suicide depends upon how well the adults are able to express themselves and create unity. The less involvement there is and the higher the level of conflict in the family, the greater the distance that children and young people will experience in relation to their caregivers. The greater the clarity and openness when speaking about and expressing grief and problems after a suicide, the more closely connected children and young people will experience being with the adults. In many families, good communication and closeness will be a process that takes time, particularly when the adults are deeply affected by the loss of a child, partner, parent or sibling.

Children can cope with a suicide – if adults help them

Research and experience show that adults often worry that such an event will inevitably leave a lasting mark on the young people involved. But although it is difficult, there is no such life sentence for children, large or small. When children and young people are well taken care of, the majority will be able to cope with the fact that somebody dies, even in the case of a suicide.

Concrete advice about how to inform and speak with children about suicide has been explained well by the Norwegian psychologist Atle Dyregrov,[13] who has extensive experience in working with children in crisis (see also www.childhoodbereavementnetwork.org.uk; www.uk-sobs. org.uk). He focuses on two key guidelines that should form the basis for helping children and young people who are bereaved by suicide:

- Everything that one says should be true – but one need not say everything that is true.

- Speak so that the children listen – and listen so that the children speak.

Some families may need family-based counselling and help, in order to improve family communication and get the family system back on its feet again. This will serve to promote openness and the family members' ability to express grief in the family. In this way, one will also avoid keeping any facts of the suicide secret, ensure that emotional and material support are available for children and young people, and motivate the adults to seek professional help if necessary. To help those children who are struggling the most, it is important to identify the need for and provide help for psychosocial problems. This is important with an eye towards helping the young people cope with the impressions and strain of the suicide and to reduce the risk of long-term consequences (see Chapter 10).

CHAPTER 7

Coping on the Road Ahead

For those bereaved by suicide who first and foremost feel like victims, it is extremely important to find a way out of the victim role. Feeling like a victim obstructs constructive thinking and makes it more difficult to progress into a coping role. Most bereaved people have a repertoire of coping strategies, resources that many do not know they possess until they find themselves in the extreme situation of losing somebody by suicide.

RESISTANCE AND RESILIENCE

A focus on resistance and resilience implies having a resource-oriented perspective, with an emphasis on the fact that most people manage to cope when confronted with severe strain. The focus is on the individual's conditions and potential for adapting to a major negative life event. This takes place when the bereaved person succeeds in moving on with his or her life in the long term, while at the same time carrying the deceased with him or her in an appropriate and helpful way. Good resilience is demonstrated when one functions well physically, psychologically and socially, in spite of great adversity and many burdens.

What is it that contributes to a good development in spite of adversity? – i.e. which factors promote psychosocial health in the context of a serious life crisis? We usually consider three main types of protective factors:

- positive personality-related factors
- supportive family environment
- external factors outside the family that support and promote coping.

These three protective factors encompass factors connected with a range of situations:

- personal qualities/expertise
- self-confidence/belief in own capacity to have an influence

77

- social support

- internal experience of control

- temperament

- hope

- stress level

- religion

- structure and rules (internal/external)

- social competence

- problem-solving ability

- ego strength

- education and professional life

- self-actualization

- family and upbringing.

We cannot go into each of these individual factors in depth here. On the whole, one can say that secure, stable emotional ties and previous experiences of coping are the most important conditions for resistance in crisis. In life crises, having a close, trusted friend and a supportive family is a big help, while it is important not to become isolated. We will look at different types of coping abilities employed by the bereaved in greater detail.

'Not a stone unturned'

After a suicide a huge restoration project commences. One asks oneself again and again why and how it could have happened. Previous suicide attempts or suicide notes can sometimes provide leads. But one will nonetheless leave not a stone unturned in the search for answers that can provide a kind of meaning and that can reduce the speculation and the experience of guilt and (self) reproach (see Chapter 5). Such a search can lead to thoughts, reflections and existential questions that many have never before considered. Such a fundamental reassessment can lead to personal growth and development (see Chapter 11). Some bereaved people find answers that they can live with to the most difficult questions; others eventually have to accept that there are no answers.

Coping strategies

Coping implies the implementation of good strategies to meet challenges and adapt to new situations. Coping also means the ability to practise empathetic insight and to assume shared responsibility. All of this is important for those bereaved by suicide. Coping entails having good personal strategies for addressing the crisis, while at the same time being able to see the needs of others, such as those of one's children or other family members.

Norwegian research indicates that: (1) openness, (2) creative forms of expression and other activities, and (3) time-outs from grief are three important forms of coping for the bereaved by suicide. Openness is a chosen way of being, while the two other alternatives are to a greater extent situation-specific courses of action.[1]

OPENNESS – THE MOST IMPORTANT COPING STRATEGY

In the comprehensive Norwegian Bereavement Project (*Omsorg for etterlatte ved selvmord*; see Useful Resources), most respondents stated that openness had been their most important coping strategy and the greatest contribution to self-help. Openness here means sincerity, candour and direct speech, about, for example:

- the pain of the loss and how one is truly feeling
- the fact that it is a suicide and that one does not hide the cause of death
- the needs one has for help and support
- the experience of how one is met by others.

Very many people bereaved by suicide have experienced that this openness had a positive impact in both the short and long term. It can have a positive impact at the individual, group and social levels, because such openness can:

- address the need for intimacy and processing of one's own reactions (individual level)
- signal the need for and receptiveness to social support and reduce others' social awkwardness (group level)
- break down stigma and prevent the spreading of rumours (social/ group level).

The way in which the openness gains a positive effect for many is expressed
by this mother who lost her young son:

> We have never felt anything but proud of Stephen. He was a warm
> and beautiful young man. Hushing up what had happened was never
> something we considered. The fact that Stephen took his own life was
> something we saw no reason to hide. We experienced immediately that
> this was positive for his friends, and for the local community. This also
> contributed to our receiving enormous support during the initial period.

Openness – meeting the need for intimacy and processing of reactions

Many people bereaved by suicide find that they can process their own
reactions by expressing the pain, and some experience that this has a
therapeutic effect. It is helpful to be able to talk about the suicide, about
painful thoughts, speculations, one's own reactions or fears about the
future, as with this mother: 'I am obliged to put the thoughts I am having
all the time into words. If I can do so, I feel so much better afterwards. I
have to talk, otherwise I will go crazy.'

Others have a deeply felt need to speak about the deceased with someone
else who knew him or her. They find that trying to keep everything bottled
up inside makes things worse and that it helps to express their feelings and
thoughts. It contributes to absorbing the reality and to the processing of it,
as this mother says: 'It is important to speak openly about the death, and
not try to escape from reality, but take the time to process whatever comes
up. That is why I must speak about him, the deceased.'

By putting feelings and thoughts into words and repeating the unreal
situation that has occurred again and again, particularly in the beginning,
the suicide eventually becomes more real. Many bereaved people need to
let off steam or simply express feelings of sadness, confusion, anger or the
experience of having been abandoned. Some people find that through this
they also acquire new insights on their own situation. Most do not so much
need feedback on this type of openness as they need good listeners, such as
this young man who lost his brother:

> It has been helpful to talk with others by speaking about my experiences
> and feelings to anyone who was willing to listen, formulating thoughts
> over and over again until one feels that one has succeeded in expressing
> what one is thinking.

When family members express pain and what they think and feel about the
suicide, the communication within the family becomes much better than

if all of these things had been held back. An adult sibling gives a good description of how the family had a need to share their pain and receive mutual support. The openness here was a means of being able to provide each other with the opportunity for this:

> One must not shut others out from one's grief. It is important to talk about how you are feeling, which makes it easier for others to be close. If you are personally open, this will potentially lead others to do the same.

Many people bereaved by suicide experience the importance of being open in relation to their partner and in this way being able to grow closer to one another in the period after the suicide. For others, this can go wrong. Mutual respect and acceptance of different ways of grieving are also necessary conditions in order for the unity in the family to be able to function. Knowledge about the fact that men, women and children react differently and have different coping strategies is important in terms of creating open communication in the family.

Research shows that it is more frequently women who feel the need to express and share thoughts and feelings, although many men also use this as a coping strategy. Although a number of men would like to be better at expressing their feelings, they are, as a group, more action-oriented in their coping strategies than women. To a greater extent women can take part in deep conversations with friends, which can be beneficial, but which can also have negative consequences if it becomes 'co-rumination'.[7]

Co-rumination

Although we do stress the importance of talking about what has happened, it is important to know that a 'brooding rut' can have negative consequences. This can arise when discussions become excessive, full of repetitions and speculations about and dwelling on problems, as a rule together with a girlfriend, friend or family member. When the bereaved constantly repeat the story of their difficulties and only focus on these, there is a risk of increasing one's anxiety and dejection. In this way, deep, extensive and repeated conversations that are intended to provide support could in fact reinforce emotional adaptation problems over time. The solution is not to refrain from talking but to have an awareness of whether the conversations, with time, lead to movement forward, or whether they simply result in increased dejection.

Openness – contributes to increased support from social networks

The fact that openness contributes to increased support from the network of the bereaved is an important consequence of this coping strategy. Those bereaved by suicide find that it is important to tell others about what has happened, how they are feeling, the support needs they have and how others can best provide support. In this way, they give their networks an understanding of the situation.

Isolating oneself can be extremely risky for the bereaved, but it is also a very common reaction in the aftermath of a suicide. If friends and others from whom one wants support don't learn of how one is feeling, the possibility to speak with others and find relief from some of the emotional pressure one is experiencing is quickly cut off.

By being clear in relation to friends and family about what has happened and how one is feeling, the bereaved send signals about their own needs and their receptiveness for social support from those around them. The people around them understand then how they should proceed, which serves to reduce the helplessness that many experience. Most find that it is a relief not having to pretend that they know nothing about what has happened, because as a rule they have heard about it from others. Openness increases others' ability to give support. By reducing other people's feelings of helplessness and ineptitude, the road is cleared for making the many resources found in the social networks available to the bereaved to a greater extent (see Chapter 8). Many bereaved people experience that this is necessary, as with this mother: 'They don't know how to handle it, so we must help them.'

Many bereaved people gradually recognize the significance of openness in the period following the suicide. Others practise from an early stage a proactive openness that entails their instructing and training the people in their surroundings in how they want people to relate to them. They have the personality and strength to take the initiative in helping others to learn how to meet them halfway. They describe how they have made contact with others, initiated a conversation, sought out others to solicit their help, invited others to their home and not pulled away; they went out and mixed with people and did not shut others out. Many young people are quite adept at this. Here are some examples of young people's proactive strategies:

In that I was able to say his name and speak about him, I demonstrated to my friends that I would not be embarrassed and react in a negative manner if they did the same.

I did not give them the chance to run away; they were obliged to listen to me and I told them about the death.

Thank those who contact you. Send signals that it is good to be comforted even if one is unable to handle it there and then.

The bereaved also experience that if the cause of death is kept a secret, they will not be able to talk about the most important and difficult questions: the questions related to why, guilt or stigma. Openness also undermines the basis for rumours.

Openness – contributes to breaking down stigma and preventing the spreading of rumours

According to many bereaved people, openness beyond their own circle of friends and family is important with respect to preventing rumours from spreading and reducing their feelings of guilt and shame in the longer term. This can be done by having social networks take part in the funeral and memorial service. The news about the suicide can be communicated through an obituary using phrases such as 'he took his own life', 'she could not bear to live any longer' or 'he chose to leave us'. Although older family members at times can be sceptical about publicizing the cause of death in such a way, they often change their minds when they experience the positive way in which others greet them afterwards. Eulogies in church or obituaries in the newspaper in which the cause of death is mentioned are becoming increasingly more common in Norway, for example.

Some bereaved people inform school classes, youth groups or workplaces about a suicide. In this way, through clear and open information on their own terms, they can break down the stigmatization and secrecy surrounding suicide, and at the same time mobilize and make arrangements for support.

Openness through the media

In recent years, those bereaved by suicide have to an increasing degree elected to step forward in the media to illuminate various themes related to suicide or the situation of those bereaved by suicide. By focusing on the deceased as well as the bereaved as ordinary human beings, good press coverage can contribute to breaking down taboos about suicide risk groups, at the same time demonstrating that suicidal processes are complex. This can also create a sense of affiliation and support for other bereaved people who do not have the strength to come forward. Many find a source of support in reading about bereaved individuals who dare to come forward and who are not ashamed about their situation. And, not least, the bereaved can derive hope about their own situation by reading about other bereaved individuals who have moved on in life.

If those bereaved by suicide want to speak out through the media, it is important to safeguard their boundaries. The message is to be transmitted without being exploited by journalists. One is to play on the same team as the media, but never be naive about their intentions. It is, for example, important always to ask to double-check quotations in connection with an interview. The bereaved should also impose requirements to see photos that will be used in the article/interview, the captions, and, in particular, the headline. Even though it is the media's duty and responsibility to prevent a contagion effect in the coverage of suicide, the bereaved should nonetheless ensure that their stories are not presented in an idealized or sensational manner.

Openness is a demanding strategy

Openness can be difficult to achieve and is not always positive for those bereaved by suicide. Not all bereaved people have the energy to be proactive in relation to their network. The Norwegian Bereavement Project showed that those who struggled the most were those who did not have the energy to reach out to others but instead isolated themselves. Others experience that not all friends or family members manage to relate to the painful experiences which openness mobilizes for them. There can also sometimes be disagreement about what actually happened, so that one is unable to present a common story to the outside world.

Many people bereaved by suicide must proceed by trial and error in relation to those around them before they find out what is beneficial for them personally. Not everyone experiences openness as a good coping strategy, and this can be because it feels unnatural in terms of their personality, because the relationship they have with those around them is not conducive to this, or because they have other coping strategies which work better for them. Below we discuss other coping strategies which people bereaved by suicide have found useful.[3]

FORMS OF EXPRESSION AND ACTIVITIES THAT OFFER MASTERY

Those bereaved by suicide utilize a number of forms of expression and activities to master daily life and move on in their lives, such as participation in rituals and ceremonies, the lighting of candles and gathering of mementos, or procuring information. Many find listening to music, writing, religious or physical activities, professional activity/other work or giving the body nutritional and vitamin supplements to be helpful.

Participation in rituals and ceremonies

Many people bereaved by suicide emphasize the importance that taking an active part in arranging both the wake and the funeral had for them. Although it can be a painful task, a number of bereaved people want to take part in preparing the body of the deceased or in other preparations before the wake and funeral. In this way, they have the chance to give a personal touch to the choice of clothing, songs and flowers, the design of service booklets for the funeral, eulogies or notices in the newspaper. For many bereaved people, this constitutes an important final message and farewell to the deceased.

By having funeral directors inform them about and make the arrangements necessary to enable active participation, increasingly more families have the chance to say goodbye to the deceased in a personal manner. When it is a young person who passes away, it can, for example, be possible to give the final farewell a youthful touch adapted to the deceased. This is also something that the family can do together by sharing the different tasks involved in the preparations. Children and young people can, for example, take part by putting drawings or other symbolic objects in the coffin. Although many bereaved people speak of how indescribably difficult it is, they are afterwards very pleased that they managed to play such a large part in the funeral. It is not unusual to hear afterwards that the bereaved do not understand how they managed to take part as they did, but that they are grateful for the support and help they received in making the final farewell personal and dignified. A mother who lost her son expresses this:

> I think that it is very important that those who are left behind are allowed to play a part in the funeral, in terms of what we like and what he, the deceased, liked. Because we are the ones who are left with this. Although what has happened is terrible, we will have something good to hold on to in terms of the last things we did.

Lighting candles and mementos

Many bereaved people experience that putting candles, photos and flowers at the site where the death occurred is a gesture that helps them a great deal. Friends and acquaintances of the deceased and the bereaved can gather there to mourn or talk among themselves during the days before the funeral. Others speak of how they seek to be close to the person they have lost and find comfort in visiting the grave or looking at photos.

> My son and I visited the place where she died every single day. We lit candles and held one another. It was unbelievably painful, but we had one another in our grief and the candles conjured up images of her. Both images of her alive and after her death. After the funeral we stopped visiting the place where she died and moved the lighting of candles to her grave. In the beginning, we lit candles by a wooden cross with her name on it. Later on, the gravestone was laid, engraved with her name, date of birth and the date of her death. It was an incredibly painful commemoration of the fact that she was gone for ever. At the same time, it was a reality check which contributed to helping us now to be able to look forward.

While a number of bereaved people derive comfort and help from relating to things that remind them of the deceased, there are others who do not manage to do so until months have passed. Here it is important to know that there is no right or wrong time, and to have respect for the fact that those who are grieving must be allowed to decide this at a time that feels right for the individual. For some, the bedroom of the deceased, as it was on the day their loved one passed away, is a place where they can seek calm and comfort for a long time after the death.

Procuring information

There is a large demand for information about common reactions to suicide, gender differences in grief, children's experience of grief and how one can support children. Information is a form of self-help in terms of understanding and interpreting what has happened and being able to move on. In that it is based on empirical research and testimonies of people bereaved by suicide, we hope that this book will be useful for the bereaved and those who seek to help them. Some people bereaved by suicide also seek out comfort and pleasure in fiction and prose, others in texts of a more philosophical, existential or religious nature.

Listening to music

Listening to music is something that many bereaved people find meaningful. Young people in particular mention that they have found help and comfort in music. We know that tranquil music can soothe the soul and promote sleep. Some people have a great need to hear music that they associate with the deceased or the music he or she liked best. Others cannot bring themselves to do so, because it intensifies the loss.

Writing

Both adults and young people can find writing to be extremely helpful. They can write about their innermost thoughts and deepest feelings, about memories of the deceased, about what happened, or about how the death changes them as human beings. They put their pain, loss and longing into words, and, in some cases, thoughts about ending their own lives. It can also be good to get anger and rage about the fact that the deceased took his or her own life and abandoned the family out of one's system and down on paper. Many express feelings of guilt and write down thoughts about what they could have done differently. Some write in a journal form about their own experiences since the day of the suicide, while others write more sporadically.

A father who felt a need to get his thoughts about his son's death down on paper began writing in chronological order. While it was the writing process itself that helped the father, his wife found it beneficial later on to read what he had written, not least as a way of experiencing that she personally had advanced in her grieving process:

> I read it when he [the husband] was out. It is helpful to take it out and read it. I sense how some of the things that I felt there and then emerge while I am reading it, but at the same time that a change has taken place.

Many people find it meaningful and healing to create a scrapbook of mementos in which they write their own message to the deceased in the form of a poem or text. The scrapbook can be made by pasting in photos, texts, newspaper clippings or small keepsakes in chronological order, from the date of birth until death. This is a way of treating the deceased as a beloved and precious memory, a memory which they can share with others who are close or who show an interest.

The American psychologist James Pennebaker has shown that writing after traumatic events can have an extremely beneficial impact on the grieving process.[4] The understanding behind this is that finding expression for feelings can have positive health effects, while holding them back can be negative. A number of studies have shown that the written word has helped crisis-stricken individuals to organize their thoughts, express feelings and diminish inner arousal and tension. To process feelings, Pennebaker encourages crisis-stricken individuals to write a story in which they express their innermost thoughts and feelings by writing whatever comes to mind and without thinking too much. Usually one writes for 20–30 minutes a day for 3–5 days, without any concern for typos or misspellings. The point is to write continuously and rewrite the last sentence rather than stop writing. One is to keep in mind that nobody need read this. It is helpful nonetheless. Today writing is also used as a recognized form of therapy, in which a therapist will instruct the bereaved in how to write for the best possible impact. Some bereaved people also discuss what they have written with their therapist.

Religious and spiritual activities
Some bereaved people find help in religious activities. Those who seek out and find comfort in religion are usually those who already have a religious faith. It is therefore relatively seldom that religion begins to play a new and significant role in the initial period after a death. On the contrary, there are more bereaved who find that it becomes more difficult to believe in God's presence, the church and the message of the Bible after a suicide. Many also find it difficult that a number of denominations condemn suicide. The position of many religious bodies today, however, is more one of forgiveness and mercy rather than condemnation. For some people, spiritual dimensions, such as asking oneself whether one will meet the deceased again or if spiritual contact is possible, assume a more central role in their lives after the death.

Physical activity
Physical activity mobilizes personal resources, promotes positive thinking and emotions, increases one's faith in one's own ability to cope with problems and generates greater self-confidence and improved self-control. Exercise liberates the body's production of endorphins, which has a documented positive effect on psychological health.[5]

People bereaved by suicide also state that physical activity is often a good form of self-help. In the Norwegian Bereavement Study more than half of both young people and adults indicated that working out, going for a walk or other forms of physical activity have helped. Although there are many women who work out or are otherwise physically active, the study shows that men more frequently than women implement some form of activity strategy. In addition to different types of physical exercise, strenuous housework or gardening are also experienced as having a positive effect.[6]

Physical activity helps to get rid of aggression and tension and counteracts feelings of physical stress or dark thoughts. Many women indicate that they have experienced the benefits of physical exercise through walking, either alone or with girlfriends. Others go to the gym or for a run. A mother who benefited from physical exercise in processing her grief speaks about the effects: 'I could be completely stiff in my whole body or full of rage when I started exercising. But unbelievably enough I felt much better afterwards.'

Through strenuous physical activity, the bereaved describe how they are able to gain a little distance from their thoughts and how the body becomes tired, making it easier to fall asleep. One man spoke of how he walked and walked for weeks in the mountains to find the gravestone for his son, while another said that the garden had never been as well tended as it was during that painful spring. Still others speak of how they built a cabin or renovated the kitchen.

But not everyone who is accustomed to regular physical activity manages to continue with this in the period after the death. During the first weeks, the lack of initiative and strength prevent a number of those who would like to exercise from mobilizing the energy required to do so. It can then be a good idea to try to start with low expectations, as one father did. He envisioned a high jump where he put the bar all the way down on the ground, while he forced himself to carry out tiny activities to jump over it in the beginning. Gradually, and as the activities began increasing his energy, he lifted the bar higher and higher until he finally managed longer exercise sessions. In this way, he gradually managed to increase his level of activity and emerge from a state of complete lethargy.

Much research has documented the positive impact of physical activity on our emotional health. Studies of physical activity in connection with light and moderate depression show both improvement and a reduced risk of a relapse. In this way, such activity can break a vicious cycle of passivity, sleep disturbances and despondency. Because the greatest health benefit of physical activity is felt in the course of the first half-hour, it is best to make the activity a regular part of daily life, rather than an infrequent, all-out effort. In other words, the greatest health benefits come from physical activity on a regular basis in shorter bursts instead of irregularly and for longer.

Nutrition and vitamin supplements

Proper nutrition and vitamin intake are important with respect to keeping on one's feet throughout the grieving process. A mother with professional knowledge about the body's needs for vitamins and minerals found that the most important thing she could do after the death was 'to be sure to get enough vitamins and minerals in order not to become depressed'. She relates here how she tried to take care of her body and soul to the best of her ability:

> There are surely many who are in mourning who just sit and smoke and drink coffee or eat cake, and then to be sure you'll hit bottom. This is terribly important, because if certain nutrients are missing, you'll hit the wall. You won't manage to keep going. I have learned that if I start to feel down, I add a little extra zinc, vitamin B6, avocado or pineapple. There are a lot of such things that increase serotonin content. And I try to get out and get some fresh air and a little exercise every day. Because I know that all of this affects the hormones and the psyche. So I do it consciously. And I am convinced that it is one of the reasons why I manage to keep going. And then I am always dependent on having spiritual projects. I have to be sure to give both my body and my mind what they need.

Professional activity and work

In the Norwegian Bereavement Study, half of those involved, both men and women, stated that it is important to return to work as soon as possible.[7] They indicate that it helps to return to as normal a life as possible, because then one can take advantage of the social network that is found at work, or work in itself can contribute to preventing too much rumination. To ensure such desired effects, it is a condition that the work requirements are not too taxing, and that the work over time does not serve as a means of escaping from what has taken place. If the employer is flexible and the requirements not excessive, it is possible to use work as a means of taking breaks from grief work. Some professions, however, require the bereaved to be on sick leave for short or long periods of time because the nature of their job precludes the required flexibility. Health personnel who have patient contact or work that entails high-level demands on attention and concentration are one such example.

The bereaved also differ in terms of the importance of being aware of when it is right or wrong to return to work. Some have experienced that it is important to be able to take it easy in a work context so as to be able to begin the grieving process. A father wonders after the fact whether he perhaps returned to work too soon and that it served as an escape: 'I worked and worked to get away from my grief. Perhaps it was cowardly, but it was my way of doing it. I went back to work after two days.'

While one respects the individual choices and possibilities of the bereaved with respect to the right time to return to work, it is important to be aware of the opportunities for help and support that can be found at the workplace (see Chapter 8).

TIME OUT FROM GRIEF
Survival strategies
A number of the bereaved describe ways of thinking or acting that they have personally discovered for themselves. A man describes with relative pragmatism how he perceives his situation: 'One must understand what has happened, gain control over the strongest feelings and let the rest come as it may. I will never forget it, but I must learn to live with this.'

A woman describes how she implements strategies to structure her daily life: 'It is important to get up every day, do the usual things; not forget the others in the family – stay busy – go out – don't isolate yourself.'

Some bereaved people experience that it helps to set limits for the presence of others if they experience this as a strain. (Some people tend to say very stupid things to bereaved.) A mother speaks of how she created a plan for diminishing her own fantasies about how and what happened. She went to the site of the suicide and read through the hospital journal. In this way, she was able to let go of all of the self-produced fantasies that she was struggling with. A father tells of how he created a safety net for himself by contacting the company physician who did not know about the death because the workplace was located far away from his home:

> When I returned to the workplace, I went to see the company physician and told her what had happened. I said to her, 'I want you to know exactly how I am feeling now, in case something or other should arise that I need help with. I want you to know, in the event something should happen, that I have been through horrible things.' She had a better understanding of the mechanisms that can be triggered than my colleagues did. I spoke with her on several occasions. It was good to know that there was a professional just a few offices down the hall who knew how I was doing, who was aware of it and who would give me a pat on the shoulder when we met in the hallway. It gave me a sense of security. So I feel that I have received the help that I needed. I have actually determined the degree of help that I had a need for myself.

Creating a time-out

An extremely good piece of advice is to give oneself breaks from grieving. Many, however, find it difficult to push aside grief and loss. Some experience having a guilty conscience if they 'try to forget' the deceased, and for others the grief and trauma is all-consuming, particularly during the initial period. In particular, parents who lose children by suicide speak of not being able to pull themselves out of the pain, or that they experience having a guilty conscience 'if they have too good a time too soon'.

Nonetheless, many bereaved experience a time-out from grief as being extremely positive when they can manage it, such as by designating specific times in the day as periods to do or think about something else. People speak of how they have been obliged to force themselves not to have a guilty conscience about giving themselves breaks, by asking themselves whether the person one has lost would have objected to their doing this for themselves and their loved ones. The best advice is to do something one enjoyed very much before the death. Some of those bereaved have the following tips for time-outs:

- go to the movies or attend a concert
- visit friends and family
- go on a trip
- seek out something or someone who helps you to think about something else – grandchildren, for example
- resume distracting hobbies, such as painting, reading, handicrafts or bridge.

Many people bereaved by suicide experience that spending time with close friends is good therapy and advise others to push themselves to accept invitations to meet with friends, even if one really feels that it is an effort. It can also be a good idea to get out and meet people at an early stage, because if one does not, it can become more difficult to do so as time passes. Some bereaved people speak of how they travelled and explored new and interesting destinations after the death. Learning about the destinies of others, both current and historical, can be good therapy. But some bereaved people warn against travelling too soon, because it can hinder or postpone the grieving process.

A key self-help guideline is to use coping strategies and activities that have previously been helpful in difficult situations.

The coping of young people

The most important protective strategies related to children's resilience are:

- those that reduce a child or young person's seeing, hearing or in other ways absorbing strong stimuli connected to the suicide (exposure)

- those that reduce the risk of negative chain reactions after any exposure

- those that promote self-confidence and the belief in the child or young person's own ability to influence a situation through stable and supportive relations

- those that open up positive possibilities.

Especially after the acute phase is over, the youngest children's reactions are to a large degree dependent upon the parents' attitudes and coping abilities. Young people's coping has many features in common with that of adults, with some clear differences.

It appears that children and young people have more rational coping strategies, in that they express a greater faith in the future, optimism and vitality than do adults. They say more frequently that one must be rational in relation to the fact that 'what's done is done', without this meaning that they are taking the death lightly. A 20-year-old is representative of many when he says: 'Done is done, there is no point in creating a theory to explain why. We will never find out.'

Young people also more frequently implement more proactive self-help than do adults. The majority of young people emphasize the significance of doing things that are pleasurable to keep from sinking into a depression. Doing enjoyable things – such as spending time with friends, going on outings, going to discotheques and the movies and so on – is experienced as being helpful in terms of pulling oneself up from grief. Many express that it is important for the processing of grief to have something to go to or to be interested in. It also appears that young people to a greater extent than adults manage to alternate between being in their pain and then disconnecting from it, as one often sees in younger children. A young boy who lost his mother describes how he succeeded in taking more active control and management of his thoughts:

> I believe that perhaps I have been a bit observant of my mental life. I have thought about not accepting certain thoughts, and which thoughts

> I will accept and what I am permitted to think about. There was a man who once said that everything begins with a thought...

Young people also tell of how they push themselves to do things that they know will help them, even though they really don't feel like it. They do so because previous experience has shown them that it has a good effect on them. Creating a time-out or experiencing 'rays of hope' is often mentioned as coping advice by young people, if one can manage this. A young girl who lost her sister says the following about this:

> Now I force myself to do some kind of physical activity because I know that physical exercise gives physical energy. So when I am tired, I go and work out. And it helps. I believe in fact that it is the only thing that has helped me, along with talking – when I feel like talking about it. When I am exercising, I don't know what happens, but the pain retreats into the background.

Other young people speak about the importance of trying to live as much as possible as before and to maintain daily habits and routines as best they can. This is particularly the case for school and free time. A girl who lost her father says the following about this: 'It is important that you have something else to do, something that is solid and that you have always had.'

About the experience of writing down thoughts to find relief from ruminations, one young person says:

> Especially if you are alone and your thoughts are spinning and you can't get it out, it is a good idea to put it down on paper. You don't write the same thing over and over again, because you've got it out. But if you just sit and think, it just goes around and around.

On the basis of what emerged in two Norwegian studies,[8] young people offer the following self-help tips for others who find themselves in the same situation:

- spend time with friends: have a time-out, have some fun, forget

- let others see that you tolerate and want openness

- find relief from ruminations by writing: poetry, a diary, letters, an obituary, songs to the deceased; create a scrapbook

- talk to the deceased – for example, at their graveside

- listen to or play music, such as something that the deceased liked

- commemorate the deceased on important days – for example, by celebrating their birthday

- think about positive experiences with the deceased; 'reminisce and cry'

- get anger out – by punching a pillow, for example

- read poems and literature about suicide

- go for a walk to think or talk about the deceased, alone or with somebody

- do strenuous physical activities that produce energy and free you from your thoughts

- get involved in religious activities

- work, including housework.

CHAPTER 8

Support from Social Networks

Support from social networks is important for those bereaved by suicide. Here we will address in greater detail what a social network is and why it is important.

THE MEANING OF SOCIAL NETWORK SUPPORT
What are social networks and network support?
Social networks are made up of close or more peripheral family members and friends, work colleagues, classmates, neighbours or acquaintances. Most people will have different network 'circles', from their closest friends and family in the 'inner circle' to groups of more peripheral acquaintances. People whom one only knows well enough to greet in passing make up the outermost circle.

Network support can take the form of support and comfort, encouragement to take part in social activities and social life, or information and advice. Further, it can be help of a practical or financial nature, or support in maintaining routines and rituals. The support unfolds through an interaction between the need for and desire to help.

The invaluable support from the network

> I believe the fact that people express concern and give support is alpha and omega. We received many hundreds of pounds worth of flowers throughout an entire year following Jonas' death. I put them beside his grave and next to his picture. Some people were unable to see us, but were able to write a few words, and some demonstrated that they cared simply through physical contact.

The above quotation from a mother who lost her son by suicide illustrates the significance of social support, but it also indicates some of the challenges the network can experience in the meeting with individuals in shock and in the throes of profound grief. The mother's statement also illustrates that sending flowers is a common and 'safe' way of showing respect and concern in connection with this type of death.

The support is often extensive during the initial weeks after the death. Loved ones and familiar faces are an invaluable part of daily life at a time when one's world has fallen to pieces and everything is turned upside down. In the Norwegian Bereavement Project, almost all parents (96%) and siblings (98%) indicated that they received support from friends, family, neighbours, colleagues or classmates.[1] It is common that both close and more peripheral friends and acquaintances send flowers, come to visit, make a phone call or send a letter. Some bring books or a poem to express their sympathy, while others provide informative materials in the form of brochures and books.

During the initial period, often best friends or close family members will offer assistance around the clock. Some will come by early in the morning in order to be there for the bereaved all day long, until the time when they go to bed in the evening, or to cook for them and simply help them exist. Good friends can be there physically, by simply putting their arms around the bereaved without saying much. Those who are suffering the most experience such support and consideration as crucial to their ability to get through the initial period. It is particularly appreciated that the network not only makes contact but also takes the initiative as time passes, because lethargy drains many bereaved people of the energy required to do so themselves.

Important and valued help can also involve helping out with children or practical everyday matters. The most important thing is that those in the network demonstrate that they truly care and make a contribution of help and support with the things the bereaved need. This often implies that others listen and show empathy and that the bereaved are allowed to talk about the deceased. They appreciate that close friends listen to their experiences and thoughts without requiring anything in return. They don't necessarily want answers or advice, except for advice from others who have been in the same situation.

Bereaved parents can experience a special type of support from young people and speak of how important it was that young people came to see them after the death. Friends can come to visit, and sit in the bedroom of the deceased son or daughter, play his or her music or just speak of how they knew the deceased. For them, it is good to share memories, and it is good for the parents to gain further knowledge about how others knew and valued their son or daughter. And it is often appreciated, although it can also be painful, if someone in the network remembers and mentions the person who has died.

After the first weeks or months during which the bereaved struggle to keep going in purely physical terms, they appreciate that good friends and neighbours gradually attempt to help them to resume participation in social activities. And, in retrospect, bereaved people often see the significance of others having tactfully and gently sought to motivate them to return to a more 'normal' daily life. Many bereaved greatly appreciate colleagues who make contact and who attempt to motivate them to return to work.

Because the need for support will vary greatly from person to person, it is crucial that the support is on the terms of the individual. A mother expresses what this meant to her:

> I have one girlfriend in particular who has understood that I have not managed to make contact when I have been in pain. From the first day, she has been an invaluable support. She has never said that I must call when I need to. She is the one who has usually called on me. She has often appeared on my doorstep to invite me along on a walk. At first we went for walks when it was dark. It felt good that nobody could see me. In addition to being a close friend, she was also close to John because one of her daughters was in the same class as John, and the two were good friends. For that reason, she also participated in my grief. We could cry together and also be silent together. We did not need to say a single word, but just be close to one another. She tolerated rejection and she tolerated that the initiative came only from her.

The woman concludes her wise words as follows:

> But we must all have the ability to understand that although there are times when we cannot understand, we can still be present – we can listen and be close. Only then do we have an opportunity to profoundly understand another human being.

Support from the workplace

While colleagues have opportunities to provide direct support and care, managers may adapt the framework of the work situation. In this way, the workplace serves as something in between social network support and professional help, and can provide both functions simultaneously. A constantly recurring topic on the part of the bereaved is whether or not the workplace has been helpful and supportive in the grieving process, and how insufficient awareness, understanding and adaptation may contribute to longer periods of sickness absenteeism and a more complicated grieving process.

Findings from Norwegian research have shown that bereaved who have received support at the workplace assess this as being extremely valuable.[2] Goodwill and understanding from both management and colleagues are extremely important in the process of resuming 'a normal life', as was the case for this woman:

> All of my colleagues were fantastic. I was allowed to work at my own pace. My manager was incredibly understanding. We had an agreement that at first I was not to accomplish anything more than come in for coffee a few times a week. Some days it was difficult even to manage to leave the house. But if he didn't hear from me, he soon rang me up. 'Are you coming in today? Or should I come visit you at home?' were questions he could ask. He did not give me any choice about whether or not I wanted to see him, only about where I wanted to see him. He cared for me and provided support and it was an invaluable help. He also wrote weekly reports to my former manager about how I was doing, but the former manager never made contact, either with my new manager or with me.

This mother had a job requiring her full concentration. She struggled with concentration difficulties and could therefore not resume working until several months had passed. While her colleagues understood and supported her, her first supervisor soon after the suicide required her to give 100 per cent in her previous position because he had felt that 'it was best for her in the long run'. The fact that she was unable to function normally at work contributed to a guilty conscience, while at the same time she struggled to fulfil each day's obligations as her supervisor wished. She was told either to work full-time or to 'go on sick leave with dignity'. This continued until her doctor intervened and demanded that she be transferred to another department with another supervisor. Bereaved individuals who have reduced energy and resources and who do not have an insightful doctor can easily fall apart in the face of such a lack of understanding on the part of a supervisor, in spite of the outstanding support of colleagues. The example illustrates how important a supervisor's support and understanding are after a traumatic loss.[3]

Supervisors can communicate care and consideration in many ways – for example, in relation to absenteeism. 'You can be away as long as you need' or 'Take all the time you need' are responses that are greatly valued by the bereaved. Such phrases signal an understanding for the difficult situation and acceptance of the individual experience, along with care and consideration from the workplace. This does not mean that all bereaved individuals will need full-time sick leave or request this, but it puts the individual in a position where they are freer to do what is best for them in collaboration with the workplace. While it is accepted that most have a need for a somewhat reduced workload during the initial period after the death, it is important that the employer is also aware that many bereaved people can experience additional pain and may thus need a day or two off work in connection with significant days such as the birthday of the deceased or the anniversary of the death. This is frequently the most sensitive on significant days during the first year.

Some bereaved individuals who throw themselves into their work can experience a powerful backlash a bit further down the line, whereas others manage to use the job situation to create positive development on the road back to a good life. Supervisors should also be aware of this and pay attention to and take care of bereaved individuals who need to slow down. While some need an offer of flexibility or contact with the occupational health service in the event of any exceptional difficulties, others will only need encouragement and ordinary consideration. For some, reducing expectations with regard to their work performance constitutes sufficient support. It is far easier to be at work, possibly on part-time sick leave, in a supportive environment which is attentive to and makes adaptations for the needs of the bereaved than in an environment where no particular consideration is demonstrated.

It is also important that the workplace understands that the work capacity of a bereaved individual can fluctuate for a long time – in fact, long after the first year after the death. Here, too, the gender differences are considerable, between men who more frequently use their job and activity to help them in their grief and women who struggle to a greater extent with disturbing thoughts throughout much of the work day.

Most bereaved people want to return to work as soon as they can, because they find that this is an important step back to a 'normal' daily life. Supervisors and the bereaved must therefore determine together when it is right to apply some gentle pressure and when one should take a time-out. It is to nobody's benefit if the bereaved person later observes, as one father did, 'I don't even remember being at work.' If supervisors and colleagues work together and with the same correct focus, the workplace can help the bereaved to move on, as was the case for this man who lost his partner: 'My job has contributed to accelerating processes that have been necessary. The job provides a structure between time off and work, between the job and rest.'

Support from the school

The school is in a special position in relation to young people bereaved by suicide, because children and young people spend a lot of time there and meet many in their social network. When a child loses a loved one to suicide, the school must get involved. Health visitors, school counsellors and teachers can be important support to bereaved individuals. How the school addresses the issue will depend upon who has died – someone whom fellow classmates knew well (a pupil, teacher or father who was a sports coach, for example) or the close family member of a classmate.

Information about the death is important in terms of triggering social support from classmates as well as professional measures on the part of the school. It is important that teachers take the initiative to help by communicating information that the pupil and family want made public. Some pupils take the initiative to inform classmates personally, but most need support and encouragement to do so. Information gives classmates the possibility to ask questions and to speak about their own reactions. This can also contribute to preventing the spreading of rumours and pushy questions from fellow pupils. In this way, classmates are given 'permission' to support the bereaved pupil based on the latter's wishes and needs.

In general, it is important to help bereaved young people to return to school as soon as possible. The school provides continuity in a chaotic daily life and creates a psychological time-out from a sad atmosphere at home, such as for this young girl who lost her father:

> I managed to hold on to the fact that I was going to go back to school. That was what was in my head – hang on for two days, because school is starting again soon. I believed that I would receive fantastic support there and so I did.

But although there is a lot of benefit to be derived from returning to fixed routines by following the ordinary school schedule, it is important for the school to be flexible about the rules for absence. It will help a great deal if the school is flexible about absences and performance assessments. For young people in secondary school, this can be crucial for their continued progress in school and for their future.

Small adaptive measures can be important if children and young people are disturbed by concentration and learning difficulties. Some will need to take time-outs – for example, by being allowed to leave class or be more passive in classes without this having consequences for their marks. Young people who have difficulties falling asleep at night, for example, will get more out of school if they are permitted to arrive a bit later and attend fewer classes, rather than having to attend the entire school day with little benefit from the time spent there. In some cases, it can be necessary to arrange internships or work placements or breaks from school for short periods of time. Others may need exemption from tests or examinations, the postponement of important exams, or the possibility of taking an adapted type of examination based on whether they manage to concentrate best in writing or orally.[4]

Understanding and empathy in daily school life is important. The interaction between the teacher and the bereaved young person can at times be problematic and it can be challenging to find the fine balance between whether the care expressed is appreciated or experienced as intrusive. It is important for the teacher to sit down and speak with the young person and to allow time for this in a private setting. Teachers must not 'descend upon' the pupil with empathy and physical contact if they have not previously had a close relationship. Even if they have personally been in a situation that was highly similar and at the same age, it is wise never to say that one understands how the pupil is feeling; instead, one should just listen, be present and show that one cares.

As far as possible the school's support and help should be carried out on the basis of simple and direct questions such as 'How can I help you?', 'What do you need?' or 'What are you struggling with?' It must be made clear to the pupil and those at home that the school will go to the greatest possible lengths to make the necessary adaptations so that the death will not interfere with the child's schooling. Teachers must state clearly that they themselves or others will be there for the pupil over time, and an agreement should be formed for how the teachers can be in contact with those at home on a regular basis and adjust any measures with an eye towards taking care of the young person. Because the need for special consideration will vary greatly from child to child, it is necessary to adapt the overall situation using both one's heart and one's head in relation to the individual pupil.

How is network support effective?

Social network support is first and foremost effective because the bereaved experience it as effective. We often hear bereaved persons say, 'Without my friends and family, I would never have managed.' Research findings show that those who experience having received good network support struggle less with post-traumatic reactions, complicated grief and psychological difficulties than individuals without such support.[5]

Social network support can strengthen the psychological and physical health of the bereaved. Network support may contribute to a longer life, a reduction in the incidence of various illnesses, a more speedy recovery when one does become ill, better coping with chronic illness and better overall psychological health, compared to the bereaved who do not receive social network support.

After a suicide, good network support will potentially diminish and alleviate grief and stress reactions and reduce difficulties (see Chapters 3–6). Good support from friends and family, the workplace and the school will therefore help the bereaved to cope better with the traumatic suicide. Network support may also contribute to a better self-image and greater optimism for the future and personal growth (see Chapter 11).

Network support predominantly works in two different ways: as a buffer or as a healing mechanism.[6] These mechanisms work either individually or together. The 'buffer' is believed to moderate the reactions and difficulties which the bereaved experience through support from the network. Direct support can, for example, be when friends make an effort to comfort, provide help in a practical sense or to be physically present or when they send flowers. The healing effect is a result of a more or less constant climate of daily care, daily encouragement, good feelings and time spent with others. This is a form of support which many have without being fully aware of it, but which is an enormous resource when life becomes an uphill struggle. One becomes more aware that the support will be there and one feels less alone. The positive elements found in both forms of support contribute to diminishing the enormous strain that a suicide represents with respect to the physical and psychological health of the bereaved.

However, how social network support works in any given situation will always be connected to the bereaved individual's personal and social resources: personality traits, gender, age, coping skills, knowledge, values, life situation, sense of self-worth and of oneself as worthy of support, and the ability to accept support. An interaction occurs of such factors with social connectedness, the characteristics of the individual's social network, the degree of one's social involvement and any conflicts one might have with parts of one's network.

The effect of network support is connected to the gravity of the traumatic incident, the type of support that is given and the nature of the relationship to the person giving the support. And even if there are many common threads regarding what is suitable, each and every family and circle of friends will have their own unwritten rules for what is appropriate in the situation and this will have an impact on how the bereaved and the network interact. How one behaves in relation to the bereaved can moreover differ greatly in a large city versus a rural village, between young and old and between groups with different ethnic backgrounds.

Bereaved individuals who receive a kind of network support that is experienced as helpful have a large advantage over those who do not receive it. One of the conditions for such support is of course that one has a network that can and wants to provide support.

The network wants to provide support
This woman, aged 27, lost her mother:

> Everyone wanted to help, to do something for us. People came by with food and bedding and helped us to straighten up in our flat. It was completely fantastic. I had no idea that we had so many people around us, that we even knew so many people. It was unbelievable – how it warmed our hearts, and it means so infinitely much in such a situation.

As the testimony illustrates, most bereaved find that the networks are there for them. A study of networks that have supported bereaved individuals confirms that friends, family and colleagues wanted to provide support.[7] The words of a best friend are representative in terms of the many in the innermost circle who wanted to do 'everything' to be supportive: 'It is important to make her understand that I am always here for her – regardless of when and where or what it might be.'

Network members in the innermost circle often expend a particularly large amount of energy in supporting the bereaved during the initial days, because they find that the need for support on the part of the bereaved is the most critical then. But changes in the inner circle can occur: new friends arrive, while old friends can be replaced. The latter occurs frequently if old friends keep their distance in the period after the death.

The members of the closest network as a rule take the initiative personally to make contact if they are not rung up by the bereaved. In most cases, it is not sufficient to offer help and then leave it up to the bereaved to take the initiative, at least not during the first week after the death. It is important that people in the network ring up or call on the bereaved and perhaps quite simply take over a number of tasks in the home for a period of time. With time, the network will discover that it is completely necessary that they take on an active role. The closest network, in contrast to more peripheral friends and family members, also usually has more frequent contact in both the short and long term. This close network experiences that the most important thing they can do is talk about what has happened, be physically present, comfort the bereaved or provide social stimulus.

Networks that provide support over time discover how important it is to allow the bereaved to control the pace of their grief process. Many become more adept at listening and respecting not only the intense feelings and sadness, but also that the degree of intimacy must be adapted to the grieving individual. They learn the significance of talking and sharing memories, speaking the name of the deceased, of visiting the grave and remembering significant dates related to the deceased and the death. Many are good at encouraging the bereaved to resume social activities, preferably activities that they enjoyed before the death. Through trial and error, close networks learn that they must not pressure the bereaved too much or give too much 'good advice' and that they have limited possibilities for being able to fully understand the particular situation of the bereaved. In addition to this, many provide practical assistance, often in the form of support for the children in the family. There are large variations in the reactions and needs of the bereaved. It can be difficult to find a balance between what appears to be right in principle and what appears to be the needs of the individual. Listening to the bereaved and respecting the way in which they would like to be helped is therefore of fundamental importance.

Friends, family, classmates and colleagues who support the bereaved over time can find that they have positive and valuable experiences through the close relationship that develops. Many develop deep friendships that last for the rest of their lives.

CHALLENGES BETWEEN THE BEREAVED AND SOCIAL NETWORKS

A father who lost his young son expresses the helplessness that many bereaved, but also their networks, can experience after a suicide: 'People learn to handle most situations in life but when sudden and traumatic events take place, we discover, as does our network, that we are completely incapable of handling the situation.'

When close friends and family members' attempts to support the bereaved were studied in the context of the Network Project (see Useful Resources), one striking observation was that networks wanted very much to be supportive but were often not successful. Generally speaking, the insecurity is greater when the network member is more peripheral and when the contact between the bereaved and the network is weak.

Insecurity in networks

Friends and family, both close and more peripheral, often admit that they experience feelings of insecurity and inadequacy in the encounter with someone bereaved by suicide. They often don't know what to say or how to behave when with the bereaved. Close to one-third think that they perhaps hurt the bereaved through their behaviour – for example, through imprudent advice or comments or by talking too much. Sometimes 'good advice' from network members can be hurtful for the bereaved. Many – who with the best of intentions attempt to give advice or to expedite the grieving process of the bereaved – can experience being rejected. More than half of the network members in the Network Project believed that they had given support in unsuitable or incorrect ways, and this was something which they did not understand until after the fact.[8]

In particular, people can experience great insecurity regarding whether or not the bereaved want to talk about what has happened and, if so, when. Should one bring it up and talk about it if they do not personally take the initiative to do so? Perhaps the bereaved wish to focus on things that are not so painful? While some people worry about invading the private sphere, others are afraid of 'destroying a good day'. Some say that in time they grew tired of the constant return of grief-related topics, and as a result now and then avoided the bereaved. This gives many a guilty conscience.

Another form of insecurity is about how active one should be about taking the initiative in relation to the bereaved. Friends and family often wait for the bereaved to tell them how they can provide support. Gradually, however, many in the network understand that they must personally make contact and take the initiative. But they understand this only after they have experienced the passivity and lethargy of the bereaved.

Friends or family members who have personally lost or been close to individuals bereaved by suicide are often more secure when meeting the bereaved. They are not afraid to contact the family immediately and are more certain of what they will say or do in the first meeting. They seek out the bereaved to a greater extent, spend time with them and meet them at an emotional level and on their own terms.

Sources of strain in the network

It can be a huge source of strain to be continually confronted with the reactions, vulnerability, sensitivity, anxiety and despair of the bereaved. It is not only time-consuming to be there for them, but it also imposes large demands on psychological strength and stamina. The network must provide acceptance and understanding while at the same time they wish to provide the bereaved with a reality check. Not everyone has the resources required to accomplish this. And sometimes the situation of the bereaved will seem to be so difficult that nobody or nothing can alleviate it. The network will then potentially be characterized by feelings of powerlessness and despondency.

Network members can also experience personal challenges in the direct confrontation with death. Some are exposed to intense sensory impressions if they personally discovered the deceased, if they were at the place of the death or supported the closest bereaved when viewing the body or participating in other rituals. Some develop fears of losing a loved one and must address their own anxiety when confronted with the pain of the bereaved. Close friends or family members are extremely close not only to the bereaved in the midst of their difficult situation but also to the person who has passed away as well. It is likely therefore that they will experience grief of their own, and therefore feel some of the pain of the bereaved.

The disappointments of the bereaved

The bereaved can often be disappointed by anticipated support that never arrives, by friends and family members who pull away, by advice and support they may receive that does not help or by support that comes to an end too soon.

Many bereaved individuals experience that somebody from whom they expected to receive support evades them by 'crossing the street' or in other ways avoids contact. This is experienced as a source of strain. Many are more disappointed by family members than friends, perhaps because expectations in relation to the family are often greater.

The bereaved understand the network

In spite of the fact that the bereaved find thoughtless remarks, inadequate support or a lack of support painful and can be hurt by such reactions, most bereaved understand them. They see that they formerly may have been too light-hearted and superficial in relation to the grief of others, while they now expect that they will be understood. Many bereaved say spontaneously that they can identify with much of the insecurity felt by family and friends. They understand very well that it can be difficult to make contact and know how to behave.

Some people may seek to console the bereaved with unintentionally thoughtless remarks. 'You should be happy that he lived as long as he did;

think of those who lose their children when they are young' or 'With all the problems that you had with him, you probably also feel relieved' or 'Jacob will go to heaven because God does not differentiate between people' or 'Now you must clear away all of the photographs so you can move on' are examples of typical comments and well-meaning advice. Although such reflections may be intended as supportive and just come out awkwardly, they can be experienced as painful and offensive.

Although over time the bereaved do not expect or feel a need for such substantial support and care as is the case immediately following the death, many would like those around them to understand more of their reactions and how long and intense the grieving process can be. Even after just a few weeks, they experience being pressured to return to normal as quickly as possible. Neighbours, peripheral friends and family make contact perhaps only a couple of times and then leave the scene. Most bereaved individuals find that the amount of contact decreases dramatically after the funeral. The bereaved miss being asked by others in ordinary settings how things are going, having others stop by and talking about or mentioning the name of the deceased.

Most understand, either immediately or at a later point in time, that when they experience that the network fails them, it is more about a lack of ability rather than a lack of will. A number of bereaved people therefore understand at an early point that they must personally take control in order to ensure that they receive the support they wish for and need. Research has shown that bereaved individuals who experience being let down by their social network attempt to reduce pain, anger and social isolation by trying to 'train' family and friends in how to provide better social support.[9]

Two sides of the same coin?

Who can we talk with? How shall we behave? Can we say what we really feel? Shall we explain what has happened? Do we have the energy to explain? What will they think of us? What if I meet someone who does not know what has happened? When is it appropriate to start going out again, to laugh and live normally? These are questions that many bereaved ask themselves.

Network members will have their own questions. Are we close enough to mention the death? Can or should we talk about what has happened? Do we dare mention the name of the deceased? Shall we bring it up the first time we see them? Who should be the first to talk about what happened? Should we? Or should they? Shall we show how sad we think this is, or will we then drag them down even further? When will they want to try to live a normal life again and have less of a focus on their loss?

Although friends and family want to be supportive, they find it difficult and demanding. They are afraid of being too pushy, and struggle to find a suitable level for initiative and appropriate forms of expression for their support. They are uncertain about whether or not they are saying or doing something inappropriate.

In addition, those who provide support over time find that it is burdensome, while at the same time they are afraid that they have perhaps been too passive on occasion. This corresponds with the experience of networks on the part of the bereaved: the bereaved find that they need support but are uncertain about from whom they can expect support. There are also many bereaved who lack the energy required to take the initiative personally in relation to their network. They must handle disappointments over anticipated support that never materializes, inappropriate advice and the fact that many disappear when the need for them is greatest. Some experience that both friends and family let them down, in terms of their expectations of these individuals.

THE BEREAVED AND THE NETWORK POINT OUT SOLUTIONS

The bereaved have many reflections about their own openness in connection with receiving network support. They point out that through greater openness about the suicide, about how they are feeling and the type of help and support that they need, the network becomes better equipped to support the individual and the family on their own particular terms. Openness is also mentioned by many as the most important coping strategy (see Chapter 7).

The bereaved will give signals

If the bereaved become more adept at giving the network signals, the network will experience fewer feelings of helplessness and inadequacy. Open communication will contribute to a more satisfactory situation for both parties. The bereaved will have the possibility to receive support that is adapted to the needs and wishes of the individual, while the network will feel more secure about the scope and form of support being in accordance with the needs of the bereaved.

To achieve this, the bereaved need to describe active strategies for making contact with the network, start conversations about the suicide and explain ways of seeking support and how important it is to invite people to visit at home. The bereaved who give family, friends, colleagues and neighbours sincere and direct feedback on their support find that they can more easily fulfil their support needs. In this way, clarity and openness can help the network to get over its helplessness. Some bereaved people even seek out network members who avoid them and confront them directly. They tell them that they want to speak about the death and the deceased and about how they would appreciate being met by others. Such an attitude is, however, not easy to assume; it requires a great deal of strength and courage resources and can of course be a long shot, as expressed here by a mother:

> It is not easy to take the initiative because you then of course risk rejection and experiencing yet another disappointment. But once I found out that somebody was avoiding me because she was afraid of meeting me. I understood then that she was having more difficulties handling the situation than I was. I therefore went out of my way to run into her, and we ended up standing there and talking for half an hour.

Others speak of how the wording of the obituary can also help network members to make contact, so they need not be afraid of approaching the bereaved. A mother expressed it like this:

> We tried at any rate to be open. In the obituary we wrote: 'He chose to end his life.' One could say that when one is open about such things, it makes it easier for others to approach you. Otherwise, it is difficult for the others as well in such a situation. People don't know for sure, do we dare…

When the bereaved are open and 'tell it like it is', those who have contact with or meet them are able to understand how they are feeling and how they wish to be met. They receive the signals that they need.

The network wants signals

'The bereaved could perhaps have asked more for help and I should have been better about offering help.' This quotation is from a man who supported a good friend who had lost a child by suicide. It highlights that members of close networks who wish to support the bereaved are dependent upon the bereaved serving as 'guides' in order to be able to support them on their terms. Networks experience that it is a time-consuming process to understand and learn this type of interaction. They learn through experience, and feedback about their support from the bereaved is crucial to the learning process.

Many friends and family members point out that improved support requires that they take the initiative themselves in relation to those who are grief-stricken. The initiative to spend time together, to provide support, comfort and practical help must predominantly come from the network members. Networks that have observed how grief and trauma drain the bereaved understand that they cannot expect a reciprocal, 50/50 type of contact, in which one more or less takes turns in taking the initiative. Friends and family members realize that they must dare to take the initiative with the risk of being rejected. They point out the importance of being available for the bereaved, particularly during the initial days, and of resisting the temptation to avoid them. They understand the importance of being patient, of being attentive and of trying to make time for the bereaved also after some time has passed. But, most importantly, all these factors must be individually adapted and structured in interaction with the bereaved and their network. This requires a dialogue in which network members personally must have the courage to be open and direct with the bereaved.

Members of different networks also point out that if the bereaved hold back about how they are feeling, this will influence the type of contribution that they can make. In order to take part in their grief, friends and family need verbal, non-verbal and emotional signals from the bereaved. Although the network knows that such requirements contradict their observations of exhaustion and lethargy on the part of the bereaved, they experience feeling quite helpless without such cues. Research also shows that bereaved individuals who are clear and direct summon a better and more individually adapted type of network support than those who do not openly express their needs.[10]

Some networks specify strategies to improve the relationship and communication by encouraging other networks to be 'sincere': 'be yourself', 'be honest' and 'don't beat around the bush'. A sincere relationship will make it possible for network members to ask the bereaved about how, when and what kind of support they want. To accomplish this, friends, colleagues and family members must make an effort to be active listeners and have the courage to talk to the bereaved about how they are experiencing the situation. They must be honest about the fact that they want to help out and be supportive, and express any difficulties and challenges they may be feeling in the situation. As one friend said: 'Be confident that you can help. If it is difficult to know what to say – that is exactly what you should tell the bereaved.'

Is there a solution?

Bereaved individuals may experience that network support can be improved by their own openness and by providing important information and managing to see the situation from the perspective of the network. For their part, networks emphasize the significance of receiving feedback and instruction from the bereaved to better enable them to take part in supportive relationships. This is substantiated by the fact that the most helpful support relationships arise when the clearest signals are given by the bereaved. In other words, signals should be given through direct, honest and open communication in the support process – both verbally and non-verbally. An observation is that the parties experience the necessity of communication about and through the support process. Both parties thereby indicate the key to better network support – namely to receive and give better signals.

In closing this chapter, we will summarize here the advice of the bereaved and their networks on how to achieve the best possible network support.

ADVICE TO SUPPORT NETWORKS – FROM THE BEREAVED
Helpful forms of support[11]

- emotional support – empathy and sympathetic insight, 'receptacle' function

- conversations – more listening than talk, 'follow the lead' of the bereaved

- advice – focus on the needs of the bereaved, the network's competency and equality between the parties

- information – about the nature of the death, normal reactions of bereaved, addresses, knowledge about support and help measures, literature, peer organizations

- social activities – activities to allow breathing space from grief based on things that were formerly enjoyable

- practical help – a broad range in correlation with the family's needs (housing, food, children, economy, legal/police, funeral director, contact with assistance scheme/school/workplace, etc.)

- routines – help in maintaining ordinary daily activities (eating, drinking, sleeping, housework, work, school, etc.)

- rituals – motivate for and participate in memorial gatherings, funeral and other collective acts in connection with the death or deceased.

ADVICE FOR THE BEREAVED – FROM THE SUPPORT NETWORK[12]

- Try to give good signals about how you're doing.

- Give your chosen support network the opportunity to participate in the grieving process.

- Communicate about the nature of the support you would like to receive, and how you would like the network to behave towards you.

- Give the network feedback on what they are doing that is good and appropriate.

- Propose ideas about other ways in which they can be supportive.

- Be understanding about the fact that friends and family members want to be supportive but are unsure and therefore need your guidance.

CHAPTER 9

Support from Other Bereaved: Peer Support

PEER SUPPORT AND PEERS

'Peer support' is support from others who have experienced a loss similar to one's own. It is support from somebody who understands the situation of the bereaved due to having lived through a similar type of experience. Those who have personally lost a loved one by suicide have a kind of knowledge and understanding that is difficult to acquire because it is to such a large extent based on experience. Those who have experienced bereavement as a result of suicide are therefore a particularly important resource for other bereaved. Peer support is also common in connection with serious illness, such as cancer, Aids or diabetes, but will only be discussed here in terms of interpersonal and psychosocial support following a suicide.

'Peers' are women and men, boys and girls who have lost a close loved one by suicide: a partner, sister/brother, child, best friend, grandparent or other loved one. Although there are large differences from situation to situation, all share the experience of having lost somebody close by suicide. A condition for peer support is, of course, that peers have a genuine wish to help and have adequate distance from their own loss and grief so that they may serve as a true source of help. In addition, the person receiving an offer of this type of help must also be interested in accepting it.

Bereaved individuals who wish to meet peers often prefer to meet those who have the greatest possible number of life experiences similar to their own. Parents who have lost an adolescent child by suicide are often interested in meeting other parents who have also lost an adolescent child. Young people in particular appear to derive great benefits from meeting with other bereaved young people of the same age group and gender who have lost somebody related to them in the same way as in their own case. The abrupt and unexpected nature of the loss constitutes a core from which a sense of community and understanding can be derived. The bereaved can therefore also benefit from meeting others who have lost someone in other ways, such as through an accident. Nonetheless, many bereaved by suicide find a unique type of support in meeting others who have also lost a loved one in exactly this way.[1] In this context, organizations for those bereaved by suicide have been extremely important.

What is unique about peer support?

It is a completely special type of support from those who have also suffered a loss. You don't need so many words. One knows how to provide a good form of support when one has personally suffered a loss.

This quotation illustrates how a feeling of community and mutual understanding arises and connects peers to one another. Because the bereaved have personally lived through the experience of what it means to lose somebody, they are far less helpless and unsure when meeting others who are grief-stricken. The bereaved dare to make contact and know what one can say and not say, or when words are not needed at all. The following six points illuminate how peer support works and why such support is important.

All in the same boat

I believe that part of what I liked best was finding out that I was not alone.

The young boy who expressed this took part in a gathering for other young people bereaved by suicide. There he discovered that he was not as alone or different as he had felt to be the case. A community based on having similar problems and difficulties, worries, feelings and experiences after a suicide contributes to putting one's world back together again. Witnessing that others have similar reactions can make it easier to view one's own reactions as normal reactions to an extreme event. In this way, the fear that one is going crazy or that one has lost one's foothold in life is often diminished. A woman who took part in a one-day seminar together with other bereaved people and professionals, puts this into words: 'It is the first time since my daughter died three years ago that I have felt normal when together with other people – as normal as I believed I was before.'

Although all of those bereaved by suicide are individuals and each has his or her own unique story, the particularity of this type of loss will contribute to the experience of being 'in the same boat' when meeting with other bereaved.

The chance to air forbidden and difficult thoughts

A great many bereaved people experience having thoughts that can be difficult to discuss with friends or family members. Suicidal thoughts, anger towards the deceased or even relief about the death can be examples of such 'forbidden' thoughts. Feelings of shame, guilt, (self) reproach or of having been abandoned or questions about why it happened are also difficult. It is much easier to air such topics when meeting with other bereaved people in bereavement groups or at seminars or meeting places, as was the case for this woman who lost her sister: 'When we meet with other bereaved, we start with our innermost thoughts, not external subjects, as we normally would.'

The opportunity to express difficult thoughts can contribute to diminishing feelings of loneliness, difference and guilt. There is one fewer secret to hide. Even better, one also receives sympathy and understanding when one airs the forbidden thoughts. Peers as a rule treat other bereaved people with respect, and it means a great deal to be able to continue giving and receiving support over time 'after everyone else has forgotten'. Peers provide support for one another in terms of 'taking exactly the amount of time you need'. The bereaved also encounter fewer hurtful remarks than in the company of outsiders who, through helplessness, may make such comments.

Reciprocal emotional support

Reciprocity is a key aspect of peer support. When the bereaved function as peers, it is their common experience that provides the basis for this. At the same time, this is also a condition for being able to accept support. Reciprocity among the bereaved has the effect of ensuring that communication is truly a two-way street and respectful, so that nobody dominates it. This differs, for example, from meetings between a bereaved person and a therapist – which will have other qualities. The identification with the pain and grief of other bereaved people contributes to the bereaved daring to expose their own grief and quickly experiencing being understood. Even without having known one another previously, one can understand and be understood, as with this woman: 'We understand one another without having to say anything.'

Many bereaved people need to express their deepest pain with somebody who has the strength to hear about it, but they perhaps don't want to release the worst of this burden on their best friends. Not everything can be expressed in words either – and the bereaved sense this acutely when they are together. Through acceptance and opportunities for the expression of pain, the bereaved gain the courage and strength to lift their gaze towards the road ahead. By observing others from the outside, the bereaved can more easily view themselves with a bit more distance. Experiencing that others are able to forgive and get over feelings of guilt, shame and self-reproach can contribute to personally being able to manage the same. Those recently bereaved in particular can find hope and faith in the possibility of moving on after a suicide when they meet peers with 'longer service time'. And those who were bereaved one year ago will see that they are slowly but surely advancing when they meet with those who are more recently bereaved.

Giving one another a time-out

Giving one another a time-out is an extremely important form of peer support. The bereaved often employ a mixture of humorous banter and serious conversation to a greater extent when they meet as peers than is the case in their ordinary networks. For many, it is easier to joke and laugh with peers, because they are more secure about not being misunderstood. They know that the others know how necessary and liberating laughter is, without it meaning that one has put the suicide behind one. When the bereaved know that others around them are fully informed and understand, it is easier to be themselves. It doesn't matter so much then if the laughter dissolves into tears, or vice versa. The others will understand. One will also be able to exchange thoughts about how to cope with a guilty conscience over trying to have a good time. Meetings with peers can therefore be extremely lively and pleasant, and not oppressive, as outsiders often believe. Bereaved young people stress in particular the importance of taking a time-out to do fun things together with others who have been through the same things as they have, to create a short break from everything that is weighing them down.

Stimulus for coping and growth

The possibilities for coping and personal growth that can be contributed by a community of peers constitute an important aspect of peers as a resource (see Chapter 11). To receive good advice and information from others in the same situation can be enormously significant. Peers have a kind of learning experience that indicates that there is no single way of mastering life that applies to everyone, but that individuals must find their own way through their grief. Nonetheless, the bereaved, in hearing about things that have helped others, receive ideas and input that they can try out themselves.

Time spent together with peers gives the bereaved the possibility to challenge their own thoughts and perceptions by discussing ways of addressing difficult situations. The latter can be significant days, such as birthdays or the anniversary of the death, the Christmas season and holidays, when one can't bring oneself to do things that are fun with surviving children. When bereaved adults meet, a frequent theme is handling and supporting their children. Many parents worry about their children and wonder if they need professional help, or they want advice about how they can personally help them. Peers who share such concerns will often be able to exchange experiences or provide the addresses of professionals. They can reassure one another or make a combined effort to acquire more help, such as from the school. By hearing about how others solve relationship problems or about differences in the reactions of men and women, one can gain knowledge and insights about how to manage the interactive problems in one's family. One can also share stories about how well-meaning friends and family members give advice about how they should 'forget what has happened and move on' as quickly as possible, and give one another helpful advice about how to 'train' networks without causing pain.

The bereaved can give one another good tips about helpful literature, addresses of peer organizations, websites, meeting places for the bereaved, addresses of good professional helpers or information about what has helped them along the way. Because bereaved individuals 'speak the same language', they will often be more sensitive to one another's views, recommendations and corrections than when advice comes from friends who are in less of a position to understand the situation of the bereaved. Peers will often also dare to be more clear and direct and can therefore serve to provide helpful corrections for one another when required. If the bereaved begin to isolate themselves from peers with whom they have been in regular contact (such as in a bereavement group or other regular meetings), they will almost certainly be contacted and helped to return to the group.

Peers – a societal resource

Many bereaved people experience that they have become good helpers for those who experience a profound loss and want to be able to help others. Contributing to improving the situation of 'those who follow' informs what has been meaningless with meaning. In this way, peer work has a large social significance, with an impact reaching far beyond that of the individual.

Many bereaved learn a lot about the causal connections of suicide after they have been personally affected. Gradually, as the bereaved learn to cope with their own crisis and grief, many begin to view suicide in a larger social context. They can acquire a focus on underlying and triggering factors that may have led to the individual suicide, such as bullying, a lack of self-confidence and self-esteem, alcohol and drug abuse, mental illness, inadequacies in the public health services and problems at the workplace (see Chapter 12). We therefore witness a large involvement on the part of the bereaved with regard to preventing further suicides, an involvement that they personally experience as extremely meaningful. In recent years, many have gradually become involved as participants in both care and prevention work, such as through organizations for those bereaved by suicide. As health policy spokespersons and by providing important input and knowledge about a difficult and taboo-ridden area, the bereaved can also improve the living situation of their own group. In this way, the bereaved can also play a part in preventing further suicides.

The bereaved also find that there is a large need for more knowledge in the field of suicide, and therefore contribute in different ways to research. Bereaved people who agree to serve as informants make it possible to do research on their situation as well as on the causal connections of suicide. Many bereaved people in Norway have also made a contribution to the validation of research results by reading through these. It has become a new trend in user research for the bereaved to take part as fellow researchers; in other words, they take part in all aspects of the research process. This implies that the expertise of the bereaved is taken seriously and represents recognition of their unique user expertise.

The bereaved also contribute to the social debate by communicating their own experiences and views through written submissions, such as letters to the editor/feature articles, poetry books, memoires, book chapters and books, or through radio and TV debates. This is extremely important as a means of telling professionals about one's personal situation, where the public assistance services fail, about the kind of help that is needed and how one wants to be approached. In particular, such contributions are important in terms of breaking down stigma and prejudices about suicide and for improving the understanding of the situation of the bereaved.

As peers give one another the strength and energy to look beyond their own situation, grief will be able to contribute to action and to the transformation of traumatic stress into post-traumatic growth (see Chapter 11).

DIFFERENT TYPES OF PEER SUPPORT

Peer support can be formal or informal, more or less organized, random and ad hoc in nature.[2]

One-to-one support

A number of bereaved people experience that they feel more secure meeting other bereaved people one at a time, in calm surroundings, perhaps in their own home, rather than meeting a large group. Some wish to have such encounters at an early stage after the death, others at a later point in time. A father tells of his own and his spouse's need to speak with another couple in the same situation: 'We are friends with another couple who lost a son who took his own life eight years ago. It was the first thing I thought of on the evening that it happened, that I had to talk to them.'

Whether one wants peer support from many or a few will depend upon what one feels most comfortable with and what feels right for the individual, for the couple or the family. The quality of the support in one-to-one encounters will be very similar to the support one can receive in bereavement groups, at informal meetings, gatherings or seminars for the bereaved. An example of one-to-one support in the UK and other countries is Compassionate Friends. Peer support on a one-to-one basis can be arranged informally – for example, by the bereaved contacting somebody they know about or by close friends helping to make such contact. It may also be that bereaved individuals who have suffered a loss some time ago will make contact with the recently grief-stricken because they live nearby, even if they do not really know one another. The bereaved can also meet other bereaved couples or individuals by professionals organizing this. A crisis team or a local religious leader who comes into contact with the bereaved at an early stage can, for example, offer the recently bereaved help in gaining contact with other bereaved people they know about. This then becomes a service that functions alongside that of professional help services.

Peer organizations will potentially play an important role for peer support on a one-to-one basis.[3] Through participation in the organizations, the bereaved will often meet peers with whom they develop a special chemistry and who, with time, can be more important to them than others.

Bereavement groups

Bereavement/support groups have long been the most common way for bereaved people to meet on a regular basis. In the Norwegian Bereavement

Project, it was found that approximately one-fourth of those bereaved by suicide had participated in bereavement groups, while only a small number of the groups were 'pure groups' – in other words, groups in which everyone had lost somebody by suicide. The other groups were mixed, in the sense that some of the participants had lost somebody through a 'normal' death or other types of sudden and unexpected death.

A distinction is generally made between three types of bereavement groups: (a) self-managed, (b) professionally run or (c) therapeutic groups. While the first two have a focus on emotional venting and mutual support and confirmation, the last has a therapeutic objective. Self-managed bereavement groups, with or without a group leader, often act as meeting places for the bereaved, serve a social support function and can be a supplement to social network support and professional follow-up. Professionally run bereavement groups are commonly led by a member of the clergy, nurse or people from volunteer organizations. The group leaders as a rule have some expertise on group processes, grief work and crisis and trauma reactions, but the groups have no therapeutic objective. This type of safe environment, led by a professional, provides an important framework of mutual support allowing the venting of feelings. Most groups that are operated for the bereaved by suicide in Norway today probably fall into this category. Therapeutic bereavement groups are often led by a psychologist or a psychiatric nurse with special expertise in suicidology, group processes, grief work and crisis and trauma reactions. In therapeutic bereavement groups, the bereaved can receive a therapeutic response to their thoughts and feelings, and the therapist has a greater responsibility and scope for assessing the individual's need for grief work or further individual therapy than is the case in groups providing less professional expertise. In therapeutic bereavement groups, the objective is personal change in an individual or family.

Some bereavement groups follow a structured plan with certain themes in a specific order. Other groups adapt to what the group members themselves want to talk about from session to session. When the group works in a structured manner, it is common that each participant tells his or her 'story', and the group leader subsequently comments on some aspects of the participants' stories under discussion. The group leader can also bring up different themes for each gathering, such as common grief and crisis reactions, the first Christmas after the death, couple relationships and children's grief reactions. Group leaders who choose the structured form often have an underlying philosophy that the crisis-stricken have a need for predictability and that most bereaved are interested in the same problems. Group leaders who choose an unstructured form often emphasize that people are different and therefore want to focus on the unique needs of the individual and that these needs change over time.

The composition of the bereavement group can be crucial to whether or not the group functions and is experienced as helpful for the bereaved. Many bereaved people appreciate taking part in bereavement groups where the participants' backgrounds are as similar as possible and where all participants have lost a loved one by suicide. The bereaved give the reason for this as the need to speak about and receive support for the particular difficulties they are struggling with exactly because the death occurred as it did. However, it can be difficult to organize homogeneous groups because (fortunately) not enough suicides occur in order to make possible the formation of such groups everywhere. Bereavement groups across a wider geographical area and involving longer travelling times can then be a solution.

The extent to which the bereaved receive an offer to take part in a bereavement group, and when this offer is made, can be crucial to whether or not they decide to accept or decline the offer. In the Norwegian Bereavement Project it was clearly expressed that all help programmes, including bereavement groups, must be offered to the bereaved in such a way that they are spared having to search for such groups alone. Although the number of bereavement groups has increased and far more bereaved people receive an offer to take part in one than previously, there is a way to go before everyone who should receive an offer of a bereavement group in fact does so. While some wanted the offer at an early stage after the death, most did not want to receive such an offer until after six months to a year had passed. Some groups address the consequences of this and repeat the offer for participation, precisely so as to offer the opportunity for bereavement group participation at a time that suits the individual. Most groups, however, do not have the possibility of offering such flexibility. This is often due to the fact that they do not have ongoing group activities, or that the groups are 'closed' – in other words, everyone starts on the same date and no new members can join during the time period that the group is ongoing. But the bereaved can also manage well without bereavement groups, perhaps particularly when they have a good network and/or good therapeutic help (see Chapter 10). And for some, such groups are experienced as being a strain rather than helpful.

The duration of group participation varies a great deal. Some bereavement groups have a primary objective of dissolving the group after a certain time period has passed, because the main objective is to return to as normal a life as is possible. Depending upon how often the participants meet and how big the group is, the ideal duration is between one year and 18 months. Others, perhaps most frequently peers, keep groups going for as long as the participants experience that there is a need. If the group eventually begins to function as an expanded support network, this can provide good support in daily life and serve as a barrier to isolation, but it should not then remain under the definition of a bereavement group. In the UK self-managed groups run by the charity Survivors of Bereavement by Suicide are all open groups where participants are welcome whenever they wish to attend. Often the first visit will be within the first 2–3 months.

Informal meetings, gatherings and seminars

Suitable arrangements will vary in different cultures and need to be locally adapted.[4] Therefore, the following are specifically examples from Norway. In Norway, through the LEVE organization especially, people bereaved by suicide in recent years have received an offer of participation in informal meetings, seminars and course activities or gatherings. These differ from the bereavement groups discussed here in that they have different form, objective, time limit and contents. This is a matter of informal meetings which county or local associations arrange once a month and where the bereaved are invited, frequently together with family or friends. While some meetings include a presentation about a related theme followed by a discussion, others are solely for social purposes, where the bereaved meet and enjoy time together. These meetings are well attended and for many people are very important as a secure and regular meeting place.

Since it was founded in 1999, LEVE has held an annual conference in which bereaved and professionals take part together. This annual conference is well attended and addresses key themes related to the situation of the bereaved, coping, help services and so on, but it also has a focus on prevention and prevention-related topics. At such gatherings, the bereaved also have good opportunities to meet others in the same situation and make valuable contacts.

Many of the LEVE county associations have annual or twice-yearly social events, such as trips and summer or Christmas parties. These have a predominantly social objective. LEVE's members receive an offer to take part in such events through the members' bulletin 'LEVEnytt' (LEVEnews) or separate notifications. LEVE has arranged special weekend gatherings in order to reach young people. Such two-day gatherings have been organized in different locations in Norway. Predominantly young people in the age group 12–25 years have attended the gatherings but some bereaved adults and professionals have also taken part. The contents of the programme have varied, with a focus on peer support and the experiences of young people, sport and other enjoyable activities, and themes related to suicide and the situation of the bereaved. The gatherings have been very popular and many young people have greatly appreciated meeting other young bereaved people in this manner.

Telephone helplines and the internet

Many countries have a helpline for people bereaved by suicide. This type of support is run mainly by volunteer organizations and in some countries this constitutes a part of the peer support carried out by those bereaved by suicide. The helplines can also function in collaboration with professionals who provide guidance for the services. While some are open 24 hours a day, others have more limited hours. The latter is viewed by the bereaved as a serious shortcoming, because there is often a need for this type of support during holidays, weekends or late at night.

In a number of countries, among them the USA, there are excellent websites for people bereaved by suicide, such as the Suicide Prevention Resource Center, the American Association of Suicidology, the Suicide Prevention Action Network USA and the American Foundation of Suicide Prevention. In the UK and the Republic of Ireland, the Samaritans play a major role as a crisis intervention/suicide prevention organization. In the UK, the Survivors of Bereavement by Suicide website provides details of support groups, telephone helpline (12 hours every day and manned by fellow survivors of bereavement by suicide) and support conferences. See the Useful Resources for website links.[5] Here the bereaved can find contact information for local bereavement groups or good advice on how to organize and operate a bereavement group. Interactive pages and the possibilities for group activities over the internet are also undergoing a powerful expansion.

In the USA, support groups for the bereaved over the internet have been tried out with positive results.[6] It is interesting to note that when the level of satisfaction of the bereaved was compared for ordinary groups versus internet groups, the internet groups had the best results in a variety of areas. Of particular importance were the availability and anonymity which internet support can offer and the fact that support can be activated from home. The internet can be used at exactly the moment when one needs it, when it is a pressing matter or when one wants to communicate with someone. Beyond this, young people have a tendency to open up about personal problems more easily over the internet than with therapists.

Is peer support suitable for everyone?

As long as they have sufficient information about the possibilities available, it is important to respect that the bereaved will choose the type of peer support best suited to them individually or, alternatively, turn it down.

Can peer support have unfortunate consequences?

As with all initiatives, peer support can have negative aspects if it is incorrectly implemented. Some professional communities maintain that year-long groups may have the effect of locking the bereaved in their grief. There can be a danger of going round in circles in the midst of grief and this becomes a hindrance to moving on in the grieving process. For some, bereavement groups can make a bad situation worse in that one must listen to the stories of others while at the same time not have the possibility to attend to their own healing process in a beneficial way. Another problem is that time spent with other bereaved individuals can become so all-encompassing that one pulls away from other types of networks. It is also unhelpful if the bereaved individual creates a distinction between 'us and them' or if one isolates oneself from any input other than that of other bereaved people. Sometimes, one witnesses that peer support contributes to the bereaved dwelling on their grief in an unhelpful way and to excessive identification with the bereavement status – an identity as 'bereaved'. Another consequence of peer support can be that the bereaved are traumatized by the intense experiences of others. From time to time, for example, one hears of bereaved individuals who drop out of bereavement groups because they cannot handle the problems and sorrows of others on top of their own. In particular, this can be a problem for the bereaved at an early stage in the grief process or at a point in time when one does not have sufficient distance from one's own grief and traumas to be able to support or meet with others.

Peer support can sometimes be experienced as unhelpful because other forms of support would have been more suitable. One hears stories about people dropping out of bereavement groups because the groups are too heterogeneous, in the sense that the group members are suffering from different types of bereavement with respect to the cause of death, or because the bereaved don't feel as if they are getting anywhere. Some bereaved individuals need a therapeutic objective in order for participation to have meaning. But here there are large gaps in our knowledge: with bereavement groups the experience is the same as for other types of peer support and assistance schemes – one hears from those who have had a positive experience with a programme, while in very many cases one does not hear from the others. This implies that knowledge should be produced on a regular basis that can be used to assess the quality and utilize the enormous resources found in different forms of peer support.

Not either/or – but all three!

Although peer support is greatly valued by many bereaved people, it does not eliminate the need for other types of support. The bereaved can have a need for social network support, peer support and professional help because the different types of help meet different needs.[7] Thus, there is a need for collaboration between the bereaved, peers, social networks and professionals. In the next chapter, we will look at the type of help professionals can offer and when it is important to bring professionals in.

THE SIGNIFICANCE OF PEER SUPPORT

In summary, peer support offers those bereaved by suicide the opportunity to:

- meet others who are/have been in the same situation
- receive confirmation that one's reactions are normal
- talk about thoughts and feelings, be listened to and taken seriously and feel truly understood
- express thoughts/feelings that one seldom shares with others
- 'be truly understood': 'no need to say so much', 'they can stand hearing about it'
- receive advice and information (on how to take control, find public help services and literature)
- acquire hope and belief that it is possible to move on (by meeting with others who have a longer 'service time')
- take a time out, to do enjoyable things, or dare to feel joy in the company of others, because they understand that this does not mean that the gravity of one's situation has disappeared
- support others – which is meaningful
- continue to give and receive support over time (when others have forgotten).

CHAPTER 10

The Role of Professionals

DO THE BEREAVED NEED HELP FROM PROFESSIONALS?

By professionals, we are thinking in broad terms – local religious leaders, police, doctors, psychologists, psychiatric nurses, funeral directors, social workers, family welfare services and so on. The professional help can include interventions such as communication of the news of the death by the local religious leader and police, support counselling, medical or practical assistance or specific trauma-therapeutic treatment with a psychologist.

The bereaved want help from professionals

Those who are offered help from professionals must wish for this type of help. The results of a number of studies show surprisingly great similarities in terms of the needs for professional help throughout European countries, the USA and Australia and that as many as 80–90 per cent of those bereaved by the suicide of someone close to them experience the need for some form of professional help.[1] In Norway, for example, it has been found that most bereaved people feel a need for professional assistance, network support and peer support, since different types of help will address different needs. Only a minority experience that they have no need for support beyond that provided by friends and family.[2]

Some will turn down offers of help

When the bereaved do not wish to have contact with professionals following a suicide, this can be because they feel that they will manage to handle the situation with the help of family and good friends, knowing that they can contact the public help services should the need arise. Some experience the death as such a private matter that they do not wish to involve outsiders. Others feel that they do not have the energy or additional strength to relate to professionals. The rejection of offers of help can also result from a lack of belief that anybody can help, from not wanting to bother others, or from having had such negative experiences with the public health services previously that this becomes a barrier preventing contact.

WHAT TYPE OF FOLLOW-UP DO THE BEREAVED REQUIRE?

A young man who lost his elder brother summarizes the needs of many bereaved in terms of help from professionals:

> There should be a team which in a way was on stand-by, ready to help at any given time if something should happen. Because you never know when you might need help. If you break down suddenly, it pays to get help in order to get back on your feet again as soon as possible…in other words, you should not be obliged to make contact personally. There are many who struggle a great deal trying to find the help that they need. A clergyman, doctor, police, ambulance personnel, etc. should automatically make contact with the team and such things, I think. They should come back several times.

Those who have experienced receiving help want stability and continuity in the support and helpers who have experience and knowledge about suicide, but at the same time a type of help that is flexible and individually adapted. Clear parallels are evident between the wishes of many bereaved for an ideal follow-up scheme and that which is recommended by professionals in the field. Here are some of the most important parallels.[3]

Immediate and outreach help

The bereaved want help at an early stage and for those offering help to take the initiative. This is often due to the bereaved being incapable for various reasons of asking for the help they need. A woman who lost first her ex-husband and then her son by suicide expressed her desperation over a lack of professional assistance: 'I thought about how I could break both of my legs so I would be taken care of by somebody from the public help services.'

This woman had been struggling for more than a year and a half after the death without asking for help, something which shows how difficult it can be to mobilize the strength to contact the public help services in a crisis situation. It is often not sufficient for helpers to communicate that 'you have only to make contact if you should feel a need for help'. For some, a suicide is so encumbered with shame that they shrink from seeking professional help for that reason, and also, in a fairly chaotic situation, the bereaved often do not know what type of help they actually need. For the same reason, a large number of the bereaved encourage helpers not to ask if they need help – but rather simply to offer it.

The offer of help must be repeated

Because the bereaved frequently have help needs that fluctuate greatly throughout the grieving process, it is important that the offer of help be repeated throughout the course of the first year following the death. Young people in particular will often turn down an offer of help to begin with, because they are protecting themselves from fully absorbing the situation. At a later date, this will potentially change. Young people themselves propose that if they refuse to accept help because the offer is made prematurely or because they do not understand the point, they should be given a business card which will enable them to make contact at a later date. The best solution, however, is that the helpers make contact again later on, as this 17-year-old girl states: 'They should have come back several times. Some people need help there and then, while others feel a need to take things in a little at a time and calm down and try to figure things out a bit first on their own.'

A broad range of assistance needs

The bereaved often experience a need for many types of help in the period following a suicide – and what one needs help with will vary with time. Dependent upon whether or not they have a good network, the needs of some will be met by the network, while others do not have a network and are dependent upon assistance from public services. Beyond counselling, advice and information, help with existential/philosophical questions and practical, economic and legal matters is often requested. In particular, the needs for specific psychological assistance and advice about how to master the situation are emphasized. Many bereaved people naturally do not know exactly which professionals or which type of help they might need and therefore often ask for 'psychological help or someone to talk to' for themselves, their children or for the family.

Help for grieving children

Many bereaved people ask for advice on how they can best help children who are bereaved by suicide. The Norwegian research Bereavement Project has shown that two-thirds of parents wanted more help with their children than they received and almost half (45%) maintained that they needed psychological help for their children. Parents want family counselling to improve family dynamics and to solve conflicts in parent–child relationships, and help in discussing their own ideas about how the children can be best cared for. Children and young people specify the need for more professional support that is directed towards them as independent individuals, on their own terms. They send a special request to the public help services to help caregivers so the young are spared having to do so or having to take responsibility for younger siblings.[4]

Help over a longer time-frame

Many bereaved maintain that an ideal offer of help must have a longer time-frame than that which is most often the case. The Bereavement Project showed that approximately three-quarters of those asked wanted contact with the public help services for at least one year, 'at least two years', 'as long as necessary' or 'the rest of my life'. Such requests were in striking contrast with their experiences which often entailed only short-term help.

The bereaved often continue to struggle for much longer than both the public help services and social networks appear to be aware of.[5]

DO THE MEASURES THAT THE BEREAVED REQUEST WORK?

The bereaved request a comprehensive offer of help that is flexible in its adaptation to the bereaved individual or the family. There are many research method-based reasons why scientists cannot 'prove' that such a flexible and broad follow-up service prevents the development of physical or mental ailments or disorders at a later date. As such, this field is comparable to many other areas within medicine and psychology in which one must also base help measures on affiliated research and the experience and views of users and professionals. Many of our recommendations must therefore be based on the experiences of the bereaved and their experiences of the need for help in the belief that 'those wearing the shoes' know best where these are pinching.

The findings from studies of specific interventions focusing on various kinds of trauma and grief support the wishes and needs of the bereaved with regard to follow-up measures. They show that it is best that help is offered early on,[6] that it is actively outreaching[7] and that it is important to repeat the offer of help over time.[8] Further, the studies show that professional help for children is important,[9] as are information[10] and individually adapted help and help for the family,[11] and that the interventions continue over a long period of time.[12] It is of particular importance to adjust interventions if symptoms of mental illness appear to be developing. Here, we are thinking in particular of psychological/psychiatric and medical treatment of depression, anxiety, post-traumatic stress disorder and complicated grief.[13]

In Norway, the Directorate of Health is working on guidelines about bereavement work in connection with suicide. A professional committee (including the first and third authors of this book) at the Norwegian Institute of Public Health has drafted the document that will be published in the course of 2011.

A BROAD RANGE OF PSYCHOSOCIAL INTERVENTIONS

As a means of illuminating the type of help professionals can provide after a suicide, we make a distinction between the type of general psychosocial help which all bereaved individuals should receive and the special trauma therapy that only a few will need.

The broad spectrum of psychosocial help entails many forms of interventions with a focus on the psychological, medical and social needs of the bereaved. A number of the initiatives do not require specialized expertise but rather, first and foremost, empathy and the ability to understand the situation of the bereaved. Such help initiatives can therefore be easily provided by friends and family when an available network exists. Other interventions require, as stated, more specialized professional knowledge. The initiatives have an intention of reducing the experience of chaos and a loss of control and of preventing subsequent problems.[14]

Emotional first aid

In the immediate aftermath of a suicide, many forms of help measures will in practice function as emotional first aid. This kind of help involves creating the most secure environment possible for the bereaved and providing appropriately adapted information. Sometimes it is also a matter of protecting the bereaved from being exposed to strong impressions, such as from seeing the deceased if he or she has been heavily injured. The organization of a calm and protective framework based on care, understanding and respect is a condition for being able to carry out other types of support measures for those who have experienced a suicide.

Support counselling

Support counselling will initially entail listening, being present and expressing understanding for the reactions of the individual. This can be done either individually or with the whole family present. Members of a crisis team, a doctor, psychologist or member of the clergy will often be important in the initial support counselling sessions. A practical focus on how the individual will manage to get through everyday life is central. Sometimes the bereaved need support in order to make concrete decisions regarding what they should address first and what must be given priority, and this applies to both important as well as more trivial tasks. This can, for example, be a matter of how one should inform the school or workplace or of preparations for the funeral and wake. The question of whether one will see the deceased (visitation) often arises in the initial support counselling sessions. It is then important to explain the visitation procedure, what the individual can expect to see and how to take care of the children.

Some bereaved individuals experience the chaos following a suicide with such an intensity that they need support in creating a plan, step by step, for how they are going to get through every single day. To create structure and control in the situation, it can be useful to take as a starting point things the bereaved person has done previously to gain control in difficult situations. A review of the series of events with a focus on the facts will often contribute to diminishing anxiety and increasing the feeling of control ('What happened, how did it happen, what was the sequence of events?'). Doing such a review together with all the bereaved can also contribute to sharing the information, removing misunderstandings and filling gaps in the memory regarding the chain of events. Professionals must not have a one-sided focus on the emotional reactions that arise in such situations, but rather express sympathy and understanding for the reactions while at the same time trying to alleviate these through a focus on the facts. A singular and exaggerated focus on how the bereaved are feeling and on encouraging emotional release can contribute to the bereaved experiencing a loss of control and intense discomfort. Professionals must remember that information and encouragement to carry out simple practical tasks are decisive to the bereaved individual's experience of control.

Information

For most bereaved people, quick access to information in combination with good care will be the most important form of help immediately following a suicide. The bereaved also express a great need for this throughout the initial period. The significance of information about what has happened, about search parties where relevant, about what will happen next, how one can take care of oneself, one's children and the family has been well documented. Information about common reactions, and support for the fact that strong reactions are understandable, common and normal, also as a rule has the greatest soothing affect. It is important to emphasize that although the reactions that arise are normal, it is not necessary to have special reactions in order to be 'normal'. There are great variations here. Neither is it the case that all the information and all the advice presented here must be communicated in the course of the first week after the suicide. Good timing is essential, particularly when it is a matter of help designed to teach coping strategies to the bereaved.

After the most acute reactions have diminished somewhat, subsequent support counselling can address psycho-educational information about the existential crisis (everything has been turned upside down, security, and all questions about justice and meaning), common trauma, crisis and grief reactions (feelings, thoughts, needs), traumatic reminders (duration and scope), variations in how individuals within the family react (children versus adults, girls/women versus boys/men) and about taking care of children.

It can also be important to provide information about legal or financial assistance schemes (if these exist locally) and possibilities for family or marriage counselling. Many appreciate receiving tips on literature about suicide, grief, trauma, self-help, poetry and so on. Information about support organizations should also be provided by professionals who are in contact with the bereaved. In the longer term, professionals discuss with the bereaved immediate versus long-term reactions, the reactions of social networks, existential and religious questions, the importance of saving one's strength and guidance on how to do so, grief in children over time, and the passage of birthdays, anniversaries and holidays.

All information must of course be adapted to the condition and situation of the bereaved. There is little point in providing a lot of information in a situation in which the bereaved person most importantly needs help in calming down, physically and psychologically. Because most people do not manage to take in everything that is said, it is important that the bereaved receive information both verbally and in writing. This type of information should be made available in hospital wards, public health clinics and doctor's surgeries, in the offices of clergy, funeral directors and in ambulance services. Before the crisis team or others responsible for follow-up leave the bereaved after the first meeting, they should provide information about local procedures regarding psychosocial crisis help. They should also inform the bereaved about any other public help services – such as health visitors for children, or psychiatric emergency clinics in the event of acute need, and practical information about how one can contact these services, or if the person in question would like to be contacted by any of these.[15]

Medical help

It is often advantageous to attempt to manage without the use of tranquilizers during the acute phase following a suicide. Medication diminishes reactions and can therefore further complicate the grieving process. It is beneficial for the bereaved to allow themselves to react emotionally and not attempt to be 'strong' and hold back their reactions. It is not uncommon for the people around the bereaved at this point to encourage them to take this type of medication, perhaps predominantly because the feeling of one's own helplessness is so painful. Being there and providing support for the bereaved usually has a better calming affect than any medication. Nonetheless, the bereaved should not avoid medication at any cost, but assess the need by listening to medical and psychological expertise and considering their state of mind.

A number may need sleeping pills and/or a doctor's certificate during the initial period. This is something doctors will evaluate on an individual basis, based on the ability of the bereaved to function on a daily basis. While going to work can serve as a good form of distraction and normalization for some, others will neither wish nor manage to do so.

Taking care of children and young people

Because children and young people are often overlooked in the chaos following a suicide, we wish to give them special attention here. First and foremost, it is important to be attentive to them, in that they are often in the midst of what is going on and observe a great deal, perhaps without the adults being aware of this. In order to take care of children, early help for the adult bereaved is vital, so that they will be able to continue to serve as caregivers for their children as quickly as possible. It is crucial that young people are given open and direct information about the suicide, that they are given the chance to ask questions and speak about and process what has taken place. The adult caregivers must be clearly instructed not to hide the truth, express things unclearly or hold back information from young people after a suicide.[16]

It is important to give young people information about what has happened, about the contents of any suicide notes and about what will happen next, corresponding to what other family members acquire. If the information is given clearly, slowly and carefully, this is experienced by children and young people as a relief and not as brutal, as adults often believe. In this way, adults can help young people to share their grief with others because they are 'on the same page' as the rest of the family. This creates fertile conditions for good family communication and further grief processing. Parallel support, care and frequent checks of what the children have understood are important in this context. For children and young people who are living with adults who have been heavily affected, it can be important for somebody who is not a part of the nuclear family to maintain close contact with them. Young people should be able to speak about their difficulties with someone who tolerates hearing about how much pain they are in, someone who is there exclusively for them and who is not personally grief-stricken.

Often, a number of children and young people are included in the help for adults in different ways, usually by the parents receiving advice about their children. Beyond this, bereaved parents frequently must personally request help for the children at a time when they are lacking energy and initiative. Unfortunately, many parents experience that underage children do not receive enough help when a sibling or parent takes his or her own life. It is particularly difficult to procure psychological help for young people, which is the type of help that parents most frequently are missing. Although many schools today have addressed the challenge and designed plans and procedures for crisis preparedness, psychosocial follow-up of bereaved children is still not systematically addressed sufficiently after a suicide.

Practical help

Some bereaved people can be so run-down just after a suicide that they need help with completely ordinary practical tasks and daily activities. This can be a matter of help with getting enough to eat and enough sleep, daily grocery shopping, practical tasks in connection with the viewing or funeral, accompanying and supporting children and adults at the viewing or assisting them in making important decisions in relation to the funeral. While some families need help with food preparation or watching young children, others can have a need to be relieved of caregiving tasks in relation to older family members. Help with physically demanding work such as mowing the lawn or shovelling snow is also valuable in periods when the required energy is lacking. Others need help in contacting public bodies in connection with the funeral or autopsy or with paperwork related to finances, legal matters or the police. Last but not least, there are many who require assistance in gaining contact with the public help services (health visitor, doctor, psychologist, etc.) when they want or need a more specific type of help. There are not many bereaved people who have the stamina and energy required to wait while they have been put on hold over the phone or to drag themselves in to see a psychologist, even after a long time has passed since the death. Alone, or in collaboration with the bereaved and their network, professionals can also help with informing the school and workplace of what has happened and what is wanted in the way of measures and information in relation to the children's classmates or adults' colleagues.

When professionals who are in contact with the bereaved at an early phase see that their network is limited, absent or fragile, they must make sure that the public help services step in, also with regard to practical tasks. As a rule, however, the social networks of the bereaved will be able to help out with the majority of the practical tasks. With regard to practical help, it is important, as with all other types of help, that it is offered and carried out with respect and adapted to the needs of the family. During the first week, many bereaved may need a great deal of practical help. In the beginning, the needs will therefore often be greater than when things have settled down a bit. At the same time, neither professionals nor the network should take over more practical tasks than necessary because practical tasks of a routine nature can provide healthy diversion for crisis-stricken individuals.

CHAIN OF HELP MEASURES FOR SUICIDE

The type of professionals to be included in a psychosocial help programme will vary, spanning across a broad spectrum in a chain of help measures as shown in Figure 10.1 below. Policemen, clergy, emergency doctors, crisis teams, health visitors, funeral directors and the personnel of schools and nurseries are usually key helpers. Beyond contributing different kinds of help, they can be important resources in relation to the workplace and social network of the bereaved. In the following, we explain some of the main duties of the more key professionals in the cluster and when it will be natural for them to become involved.

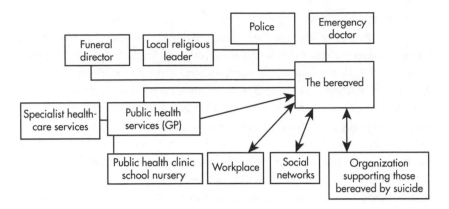

Figure 10.1 Chain of help measures for suicide

The police

In many countries, the duties of the police are connected to a responsibility decreed by law to investigate the circumstances surrounding that which by law is defined as death by unnatural causes (sudden, unexpected), in order to establish to the extent possible whether the death was the result of a self-inflicted injury or due to illness, accident or murder. The police are therefore involved as a matter of routine in connection with a suicide and are often the first to arrive at the scene of the death. Beyond turnout at the scene, their duties are connected to notification (in Norway often delegated to a member of the clergy), investigation and securing of evidence and any initiative for an autopsy. In this work, the police as a rule meet the close bereaved. Beyond speaking with the bereaved in order to acquire information about the circumstances surrounding the death, the police often give the bereaved some factual information about the suicide. The need for information will be particularly great if the deceased has been missing for a period of time and is found in a location outside the home. It is important that the police have such conversations with the next of kin and that the information communicated is honest, direct and respectful.

The duties of the police usually come to an end when the circumstances surrounding the death have been clarified and the reports have been written and sent to the coroner. On the basis of the express wishes of the bereaved for rapid and automatic assistance, it is extremely important to have routines established for the notification of a follow-up unit by the police. This unit can be a crisis team who will then contact the bereaved and ensure that the needs for help are covered in both the short and long term.

Religious leaders

Although the police have the formal responsibility for notifying the next of kin, they often delegate this to the local religious leader on duty. (It should be noted that this system applies to Norway, and that other countries will have other practises.) The leader will be rung up by the police and receive information about the name, age and address of the deceased. The leader will then usually visit the home of the next of kin to notify them. Only in exceptional circumstances − in the event that it takes a long time to reach the home of the next of kin − will it be necessary to do this over the phone. If possible, the local religious leader who will notify the family should also take responsibility for the funeral so as to provide continuity in the contact with the bereaved. Beyond notification, prayer services, grief counselling before the funeral/burial, viewing/visitation, the funeral/burial and the interment of the urn are commonly duties carried out by a religious leader after a suicide. A religious leader may also provide information about local follow-up services for the bereaved.

With Christian and other religions' former condemnation of suicide in mind, we hope that most religious leaders emphasize conveying a non-judgemental attitude in their meeting with the bereaved. The leader of the service will usually invest a great deal of work in ensuring that the ceremony is performed with sensitivity and is meaningful for those who were close to the deceased, and good support counselling often can be provided by a local religious leader. Today it is also far more common to be flexible in relation to the wishes of the bereaved in terms of songs, music and in the dressing of the deceased. In this way, the leader of the service can carry out a number of important functions in making the final farewell as dignified and meaningful as possible for the bereaved.

Emergency doctors

Medical staff from the emergency department may be summoned and will often be at the scene along with the police and clergy. The doctor's duties are to establish the cause of death and write out the death certificate (the doctor's declaration of death). Usually the bereaved will have their own general practitioner address any further medical follow-up, such as a doctor's certificate for physical ailments, sleep disorders or psychological reactions such as anxiety, agitation and depression. The general practitioner should also have a clear understanding of other care measures and ensure that the bereaved are informed or receive help to gain contact with different schemes if others do not. It is important for the general practitioner to distinguish between normal reactions to an extreme event and symptoms of mental illness, and extended grief and normal grief. The general practitioner must monitor the bereaved so as to disclose at an early juncture whether they have symptoms of post-traumatic stress or complicated grief. In such cases, it is necessary for the general practitioner to refer the bereaved to the specialist health services.

The funeral director

The duties of funeral directors involve transport, preparation and visitation of the deceased and arrangements for and implementation of the funeral ceremony. They can provide important advice in connection with the writing of the obituary or what will be said during the ceremony. Further, they will discuss with the bereaved whether they would like a memorial service after the burial/cremation, the type of music one should choose and about whether the death notice is to be published before or after the burial/cremation.

In connection with the practical tasks to be addressed, a skilled funeral director can provide helpful support counselling for the deceased. Many funeral directors have found that it is important to emphasize openness in the matter of a suicide, so that any speculation and rumours can be prevented. If the bereaved are open about what lies behind the death, the openness serves as an 'invitation' to social networks to participate. Many funeral directors therefore advise openness and advise against a funeral 'on the quiet'.

The funeral director can also motivate the bereaved to take part in rituals and include the children after having first informed them of what is going to take place and ensuring that their needs are addressed throughout. Funeral directors often feel responsible for giving those who appear to be in need of help referrals to relevant professionals. Unfortunately, they often experience that this can be time-consuming and difficult and that they lack knowledge about who can best help the bereaved with the particular needs they might have. Like the police, they emphasize a need for psychosocial follow-up that is more automatic, as stated by this funeral director with long-term experience with the bereaved by suicide: 'There is no system that automatically takes care of the next of kin…it is impossible to find the right person, somebody who says that this is our job.'

Crisis teams

A crisis team is a unit that can coordinate or carry out further follow-up measures after the police, local religious leader and funeral director have fulfilled their functions. More and more municipalities in Norway have organized such teams. These may be a typical Norwegian phenomenon, but different countries will to different degress have taken responsibility for the organization of professional help. The way this is taken care of will relate strongly to the respective culture, how suicide is looked upon, and the welfare system in the given culture. A crisis team is intended to function as an available emergency preparedness group, which the local authority has appointed as responsible for psychosocial follow-up after crises and catastrophes. The team is made up of professionals who can provide information about help measures (police, religious leader), professional helpers with special and relevant help-related expertise (physicians, psychiatric nurses, public health nurses, psychologists/psychiatrists, clergy/religious leader, social workers) and institutions and public bodies that will play a central role in connection with a critical event (the hospital emergency department, the church). The responsibilities are a part of these professionals' ordinary service duties so that it is only the organization of these that is different. The primary responsibility for such preparedness in Norway lies with the district medical officer, but assignment of the manager function can vary. The manager function is often assigned to the chief medical officer, the police, a local religious leader or others who have key duties in terms of psychosocial follow-up in the municipality.

Beyond having contact with the affected parties, the role of the team is to implement and coordinate necessary measures in the short and long term. In some municipalities, the professionals in the crisis team will assist the bereaved directly, while in other municipalities the team functions exclusively as a coordinating body which mobilizes different measures, as described previously. The particular helpers that are mobilized will vary according to the type of help required.

Therapeutic help for trauma

While a broad spectrum of help measures should be offered to all bereaved individuals (as shown in Figure 10.1), therapeutic help for trauma will only be implemented in the event of a need for further and a more specific type of help.[17] If the chain of help measures functions ideally, a crisis team, general practitioner or other professionals will identify such special needs and help the bereaved to come into contact with therapists who have the relevant expertise. If friends and family members notice that the bereaved are struggling and know that they are not getting help from the public health services, they can motivate them to seek such help or, with their consent, seek it for them. In order to ensure that the bereaved and the network will be better able to understand what professionals can contribute, we discuss below when such help can be relevant and how the bereaved can be helped.

When is therapeutic help for trauma needed?

Grief, privation and longing are common after most deaths. In connection with a suicide, the bereaved can also struggle with intense flashbacks, self-reproach, ruminations, anxiety or family-related difficulties. In general, we would maintain that there is cause to bring in more help when:

- the reactions do not diminish or disappear with time but continue with unabated intensity

- the bereaved person does not function at work, in school or during his/her free time

- the bereaved person isolates him/herself from his/her surroundings

- the family is struggling with the distribution of roles, internal conflicts or other types of family issues

- the bereaved or others become aware of clear danger signs (such as increased alcohol consumption or drug abuse/self-medication)

- the grief continues beyond the initial months without change, does not commence at all or other signs of complicated grief

- the parents need counselling on how to handle their children's situation

- the interaction with social networks has 'hit the wall', the bereaved isolate themselves or need help handling 'social ineptitude'.

Other reasons for seeking help can be if the bereaved individual expresses abnormally strong self-reproach regarding what he or she should have thought, said or done, should not have thought, said or done, has strong feelings of worthlessness or has a strong and persistent fear of another catastrophe. There can also be cause to seek more help if over time the amount of sleep the bereaved is getting is greatly diminished due to nightmares, or if the bereaved has difficulties falling asleep, wakes early or continues to brood and think about the death without room for any other thoughts.[18]

What is therapeutic help for trauma?

Therapeutic help for trauma is therapy after traumatic events. Because suicide represents both trauma and grief, the therapeutic help will be combined with treatment methods from both fields. This entails specialized help that is carried out by psychologists, psychiatrists or others with the expertise required to treat people who have special or long-term problems following traumatic events. Examples of such problems can be depression, complicated grief reactions or post-traumatic stress disorder, as described previously. The implementation of therapeutic help for trauma should be based on screening (questionnaire testing) and/or clinical findings that indicate that such help is necessary.

Some patterns of experience have become evident with respect to the impact of therapeutic help for traumatic grief. The effectiveness appears to be best documented for those who experience complicated grief and who personally feel that they have a need for professional help.[19] This effectiveness is not found with those who experience ordinary grief, so that the potential for positive effects with trauma therapy is greater the more serious the problems are.

Trauma and grief therapy are focused on the symptoms that constitute the core of the bereaved person's problems. Therapists have moved from 'just' talking to a systematic use of a series of methods, the objective of which is to reduce the problems with which the bereaved is struggling. The specialized help can entail different so-called cognitive techniques. These are methods in which the therapist works actively together with the bereaved to change thoughts, feelings and behaviour by having the bereaved practise, little by little, confronting situations that they would prefer to avoid, learning to control unwanted thoughts and feelings and so on. Training in self-help methods also is central. The psychotherapeutic help can help the bereaved to:

- take control over invasive memories

- sleep better

- master avoidance reactions

- learn relaxation techniques and other self-help methods

- return to painful places or resume painful activities

- come to terms with an understanding of what led up to the suicide.

Along with promoting acceptance of the loss and resumption of daily life, image visualization, reviewing the sequence of events, acquiring factual information, conversations with or writing to the deceased and confrontation with memories are other methods used. Experience shows that the combination of these methods is particularly beneficial. Cognitive methods appear to be particularly effective when a bereaved person is struggling with guilt and hindsight or has other repetitive thoughts that are the cause of excessive rumination. Here, therapists employ thought-stopping methods, distraction methods, writing methods focused on the repetitive thoughts and so on. Such cognitive strategies can help the bereaved to identify and replace erroneous ideas or irrational thought systems and to produce thoughts to counter self-reproach and rumination. With the help of such methods, the therapist can help the bereaved to reorganize life values and life goals, change their perspective about the event and re-establish their experience of control in life.

Research has shown that there is a relatively large risk of the bereaved developing complicated grief, post-traumatic stress disorder and more general health problems after a suicide.[20] Along with documentation indicating that it is too few rather than too many who receive therapeutic help for trauma after traumatic death, this indicates that many more would in all likelihood benefit from this type of help after a suicide.[21] Here are a few examples of what the help can entail.

Help with complicated grief

When the life of the bereaved is dominated by intense feelings of loss or longing, and this has continued with undiminished intensity for many months, it is important that they then receive help in controlling their grief. Psychotherapeutic help will then involve conversations about the significance the deceased has had in the life of the bereaved and to create some perspective about what has happened, frequently parallel to a discussion and exploration of the ties between the bereaved and the deceased.

The bereaved is asked to begin to limit the amount of time that he or she spends absorbed with thoughts and memories of the deceased. This can be done by allocating a specific time each day, such as half an hour or an hour, to think about and/or write about the deceased. For some, this is combined with their being encouraged to clear out clothing and possessions, gather these in a specific place in the house or apartment and force themselves to visit the grave less frequently. To help them succeed in reducing the amount of time they use on thoughts and activities related to the deceased, they learn different methods that give them better control over their thoughts, such as thought-stopping methods, distraction methods and different methods for falling asleep.

Different writing activities can play a particularly important role in the processing of complicated grief reactions. Some of the bereaved are asked to write about everything that they perhaps did not have the chance to say to the deceased because the death happened so suddenly. This can be writing done individually, but the family can also be asked to collaborate in writing a letter to the deceased, with specific instructions about the importance of listening to one another. In such letters or diaries the bereaved can be asked to write about:

- What has happened lately?

- What do I miss the most?

- What has the deceased meant to me?

- What am I angry or disappointed about?

- What will I always carry with me in terms of what the deceased has meant to me?

If the bereaved person is experiencing strong feelings of self-reproach or guilt, through the use of specific questions and a systematic review of what the individual knew at different times, the therapist can change the emotional logic of the bereaved from within.[22]

Help with post-traumatic stress disorder

Measures will depend upon what it is that is disturbing the bereaved the most. If this is invasive images, there are simple visualization methods that can be tried initially as self-help methods in order to help the bereaved gain control over the disturbing images. The bereaved can also gradually be exposed to the stimuli that are the most common traumatic triggers and learn to control memories and thoughts. This can be done using thought-stopping methods, distraction methods or writing methods that focus on the repetitive thoughts. For avoidance reactions, going through the sequence of events, acquiring factual information, conversations with or writing to the deceased and the confrontation of the memories and situations that are being avoided will constitute important contents of the therapy. Although physical agitation is often diminished after one has acquired control over invasive memories or thoughts, some people also need to learn methods by which to moderate physical agitation, something which can also lead to sleeping more deeply.[23] When strong feelings of guilt are involved, special methods from cognitive therapy are particularly effective for diminishing guilt and hindsight, reducing erroneous thoughts and producing thoughts to counteract self-reproach and rumination.

From time to time, one sees that grief in young people is 'put on hold' following the suicide of a parent or sibling, and in some cases young people must in fact wait until they are adults before they become receptive to receiving help. If grief fails to appear and at the same time the bereaved individual is not functioning in life, it can be difficult to arrive at a position from which to provide help, also because there is little experience of discomfort. In such cases, the therapist will emphasize relationship building to motivate the bereaved by informing them about common grief reactions, what others have done to improve their situation and what must be done in therapy in order to feel better. The introduction of self-help methods at an early stage will also be important here.

Help with family problems

Because complex family dynamics can frequently be activated by a loss,[24] advanced help for the family can be necessary. We are thinking especially of difficulties associated with how information is shared in the family and what takes place within the interaction. How are facts and feelings shared in the family? How flexible are family members in terms of reallocating roles? Who defines the story that is told about what happened? Are some members 'cut off' from others? How is the capacity for listening?

When poor family communication and unity is the starting point for seeking help, different family therapy approaches are used. By making communication, role allocation, thoughts, feelings and conflicts a part of the sessions with the family, it will be possible to establish a good climate for handling the grief in the family. An open discussion about such topics can lead to more conscious choices about how this can be handled in the family. In the family work, it is important to create open, honest and inclusive communication in which the children are involved, so that when they later readdress the death in different periods of their childhood and adolescence, they will have a solid factual basis for their increasing understanding. As mentioned earlier, it is important to help parents to reach as quickly as possible a place from which they can be good caregivers for their surviving children. Through therapy sessions, family unity can be strengthened and new conflicts avoided.

A FAMILY THAT WAS VERY SATISFIED WITH THE HELP THEY RECEIVED

In the Norwegian Bereavement Project, the bereaved were asked what would be ideal help after a suicide. One of the interviewed families replied: 'It must be like the help we have received.' The help that this family received can serve as an example of a municipality with good emergency preparedness.[25] A year and a half after the death, the parents described the important aspects of the help that they received after their teenager shot herself:

The mother heard the shot and found her daughter shot and lying in a pool of blood. A younger brother was also in the house. The mother rang the emergency number. The medical emergency call centre (the emergency department) notified a clergyman, the police and a doctor. The call centre asked the mother not to hang up – talked with her calmly and asked her to go back again to check whether the young girl was still alive. They were concerned about how the younger brother was doing and asked the mother to hold him. The call centre and mother remained in contact until the ambulance arrived (15 minutes), while the call centre continuously informed her of where the ambulance was. The mother said: 'So at all times I was in control.'

The doctor contacted the district nurse and psychologist. They arrived in the evening. The nurse continued coming every day up until the funeral, even though it was a holiday. She talked with the family and let them talk. Caring for the brother was a central focus at all times.

The parents had a scheduled session with the psychologist once before the funeral. The mother reacted to the fact that the psychologist asked whether they needed help: 'Of course we did! But we could have easily said no, we don't need help, we will manage.'

Both the mother and father continued to have contact with a psychologist and psychiatrist for a year and a half, but less frequently towards the end of this period. The mother treated with EMDR (eye movement desensitization and reprocessing – a trauma therapeutic technique) to stop invasive images and thoughts stemming from the moment when she found her daughter. The psychologist provided help in sorting out feelings and thoughts which the bereaved were unable to put in place for themselves, which helped them to move on. The younger brother was in contact with the educational psychology services, but terminated this contact after about one year.

Doctor's appointments were scheduled for both parents immediately and new appointments scheduled each time. They were also told clearly that they had only to call should the need arise. In the beginning, the visits to the doctor were more frequent; a year and a half later, the visits took place about once a month. The parents had double sessions – in other words, two sessions of 15 minutes each time. 'But it has happened that we sat there for up to a whole hour and we don't feel as if we are sitting on pins and needles and have to hurry because we have to leave right away.' During the sessions, they talked together and they were given medication and doctor's certificates for sick leave as needed.

The police helped with formalities in relation to the circuit judge and closing of bank accounts. The mother said: 'It was very important to receive this kind of help, because we had no idea about how to do it and so we were spared having to run around to different offices to get things done.'

The clergyman came to visit them at home many times. He was a wonderful clergyman, who gave an excellent speech at the funeral. He provided bereavement support and counselling. Both the parents and the brother were allowed to influence the planning of the funeral to a very large extent.

The funeral agency washed and cleaned up all of the blood and informed the parents that blood could have leaked through the floor. The district nurse informed them that there was a fund they could apply to through the social welfare office to cover the costs of this type of repair. The district nurse notified the municipal caretaker who came and did the repairs. The paperwork and all the practical details were dealt with without the family having to bother with these.

The family was asked whether they wished to take part in a bereavement group just after the death. They felt that it was too early and declined. But now, a year and a half later, the mother feels that she would like to do so if she received such an offer again.

The clergyman, doctor, district nurse and health visitor were in the process of starting up a crisis team when the death took place. The mother now sat with their brochure in her hand.

The entire town, the school and the class, the friends of the deceased and youth club did their part, as did neighbours, colleagues from the parents' workplaces and the parents' friends. The family provided less support.

THE REQUISITE HELP MUST BE ENSURED FOR THE BEREAVED

Whereas with illness there are often fixed routines in the public health services that also provide the possibility for making an assessment of the needs for follow-up after a death, this occurs less frequently in connection with sudden death. Because sudden death may result in long-term problems for the bereaved, professional help should be brought in at an early stage and automatically.

The need for established procedures

As we have seen, measures for those bereaved by suicide can involve a number of local bodies. In order to ensure that the chain of help measures and help services function, procedures for such help must be systematically organized and established. For this reason, increasingly more municipalities in Norway have developed procedures for follow-up after crises and catastrophes, and some have specific procedures for suicide. Research findings show that such procedures must contain detailed descriptions of plans for the organization, form and contents of the help.[26]

The immediate help can be provided either by ambulance personnel, a local religious leader or a local crisis team being activated for the family. One of the largest challenges facing professionals is identifying those who are struggling with more specific problems such as complicated grief or post-traumatic reactions. This will require that the helpers create systems that intercept those who need such help through an overview of what is required and a broad spectrum of help services for everyone. For both types of help, the helpers must have knowledge about suicide, grief and crises in order for the help to be adequate.

The balance between professional help, network help and own resources

It is important that professional help does not infringe upon the individual's personal integrity but rather is help towards promoting increased coping, self-care, empowerment and responsibility. The helpers must act in relation to the resources of the bereaved and contribute on their terms and not over-treat or pathologize when personal resources exist. Self-help advice is therefore extremely important. The amount of support and care offered by professionals will depend upon the individual's situation and resources and the support available from those around them.

CHAPTER 11

Grief, Growth and Development

Many bereaved people have a need to understand what is happening when one grieves. At the same time, the grief process can be affected by how the bereaved individual understands it – for example, if one expects grief to have clear phases and that it is experienced identically by everyone. There is, however, no common and 'normal' way of grieving – rather, there are as many ways of grieving as there are bereaved people.

WHAT IS GRIEF?
How grief is manifested is related to a number of factors that have been addressed earlier in this book. In spite of the differences, the grieving process nonetheless often has a number of main features and some grieving processes seem more expedient than others.

Some have only minor reactions
Most people will go through different types of grieving processes but research shows that up to 20 per cent do not feel intense grief right after the death or later. This is the case even when the deceased is a child.[1] This demonstrates that not everyone experiences grief or needs to process grief in order to move on with life. The absence of grief is therefore not necessarily disadvantageous or a result of grief being repressed (see Chapter 4 about complicated grief). In order to determine whether the bereaved person is pushing his or her grief away or is among those who 'take it lightly', it is important to look at how the person is doing in daily life. In general, one can say that if the person in question sleeps, eats, works/manages schoolwork and takes part in social activities in the way he or she did previously, there is little cause for concern.

For bereaved individuals who have grief reactions that are neither intense nor long-term, it is of course completely wrong to force them to conform to a pattern that prescribes other types of reactions or insists that they should process grief in a specific way. If health personnel, family and friends expect them to exhibit specific reactions, the pressure can be enormous and create problems for the bereaved, because they can begin to believe that they are reacting abnormally. In such situations, the expectations of those around them and of professionals may contribute to creating problems. For bereaved individuals who experience the loss in this way, it is important to remember that it is fully legitimate to continue with one's life as before, to be involved in one's surroundings, i.e. community, social networks and life in general, and live the most active life possible.

OLD THEORIES ABOUT GRIEF
Grief in phases

For several decades up to the beginning of the 1990s, the phase theory of grief was prevalent among grief theorists. This theory applied to grief following death in general. Many are familiar with terms such as the shock phase, the denial phase, the reaction phase or the reorientation phase, in which the understanding is that grief follows a succession of specific phases or stages in a characteristic pattern and within a specified time-frame.[2] Many continue to use these terms to characterize the grief that they themselves or others are experiencing. Because many of today's professionals have learned these phase or stage models and they are still found in a number of textbooks, unfortunately many bereaved people still encounter statements such as 'Now you are in the denial stage'. The reactions of the bereaved individual are then put in a context of assessment as to whether he or she is in the right phase or not. This may be experienced as lacking in empathy, invasive, insensitive or hurtful.

Phase theories of grief are not confirmed by studies which have monitored the bereaved over time. These theories are too static and there is too little focus on fluctuations and variations in grief. The majority of bereaved people, however, can identify with some aspects of the different phases – for example, shock reactions in the period just after the death and the period during which one later absorbs what has happened. In the longer term, most manage gradually to lift their heads and begin to address the responsibilities in their lives. But even such a general description does not apply to everyone.

The phase theory can also lead one to think that when one has arrived at the final phase, one has reached the end of the road of grief. In reality, many experience that they will do well for periods of time and then once again experience intense grief. Many things and thoughts can trigger grief so that it can vary greatly, even in the course of a single day. Connecting grief to clear-cut phases is therefore not only wrong in relation to the grief of an individual, but it can also lead to pressure and expectations from those around the bereaved person to follow a specific pattern from A to Z. As a rule the reality is far more mercurial than this.

Grief as work

'Grief as work' is another concept that has dominated ideas about grief.[3] Grief work implies that the bereaved must go through an emotional process in which they are confronted with the loss, go through what happened before and during the death and focus on the memories of the person they lost. The final objective of the grief work is gradually to disconnect from the deceased. In its most extreme sense, this means that one must personally make an effort in order to get through grief, and that grief is something that one must be dealt with in order for life to go back to the way it was before. It is necessary to work through grief. The focus is on the death and the loss, and the objective is to put this behind one and move on by severing the ties.

This way of thinking has been modified in more recent theories because most bereaved neither can nor wish to be rid of the memories of their loved one. Research has also shown that if one develops a personal space for the deceased in which the deceased can occupy a positive position in one's inner life, this can in fact contribute to diminishing problems after a death.[4] Many bereaved people find that life will never be as it was before the death, but that it is possible to continue living in new ways. The two concepts of grief mentioned here have too little focus on how people vary, adapt and gradually change through grief, while at the same time carrying with them the person they have lost. More recent grief theory has attempted to rectify this.[5]

MORE RECENT CONCEPTS OF GRIEF – THE DUAL PROCESS MODEL

The Dutch research group led by psychologist Margaret Stroebe has developed what they call the dual process model of coping with bereavement.[6] This model has incorporated and developed previous theories and corresponds better with the actual reality of bereaved individuals.

Everyday life experience

Loss-oriented
Grief work
Intrusion of grief
letting go-continuing-relocating bonds/ties
Denial/avoidance of restoration changes

Restoration-oriented
Attending to life changes
Doing new things
Distraction from grief
Denial/avoidance of grief
New roles/ identities/ relationships

oscillation

Figure 11.1 The dual process model of coping with bereavement

Oscillation between loss and restoration

The dual process model highlights how the bereaved oscillate between two processes (Figure 11.1). One of the processes concerns relating to and working with the emotional aspects of the loss. In the second process, one relates more proactively to the new situation following the loss. Stroebe's research group describes how important it is to be able to oscillate between the two processes – loss-orientation and restoration-orientation – throughout the entire grief process. A balanced oscillation makes it possible to cope with the death in constructive ways by managing to approach what has happened and then 'reporting back' to life again afterwards. This takes place when the bereaved person alternates between crying, talking about and remembering the deceased (confronting) and trying to distance themselves from grief (avoidance/time out) in order to resolve the challenges of the new existence without the person one has lost. It is thus not a matter of either being in the loss or reaching forward towards the new life but of a movement back and forth between these two. If the bereaved individual manages such a balanced oscillation between being in the loss and reaching out towards the new life, it is likely that he or she will experience a more simplified grief process.

　　Restoration or reorientation can entail resolving challenges of a practical/financial nature, rectifying loneliness and ruptures in one's social life or addressing tasks that were performed by the person who is now gone. In addition to the individual's personal coping resources, the interaction of the bereaved person with their social network is of significance for the grief process.[8] The network will be able to support these processes in different ways with respect to whether the bereaved is working with emotional aspects of the loss or has an orientation towards looking forward in life. The dual process model as a perspective for understanding grief therefore includes to a greater extent the significance of the surroundings of the bereaved in the grieving process. For many bereaved people, the most important thing in the beginning can be empathy and compassion, while, with time, input and support regarding how to move on in life without a spouse, girlfriend/boyfriend, parent or child can be just as important.

Creating an internal memory

In the processing of a loss, it is of particular importance to note that more recent research shows how meaningful it is for many bereaved to develop and maintain an internal memory or internal representation of the deceased. From being a person external to the bereaved, the deceased will now become a 'person' in their internal space. In this way, the deceased can remain an active part in their emotional life in the future, and have a constructive role, such as in the manner of an 'inner helper' or advisor. It is accordingly not necessary to undo and get rid of the ties to the deceased, as a number of professionals have maintained previously. The bereaved can carry the deceased with them internally in a meaningful way.[9] Nonetheless, we sometimes see that this type of connection to the deceased can create problems if it becomes too strong and prevents the bereaved from involvement in their own life here and now.[10] If this has an impact on daily functioning over time, it is of course a cause for alarm and professional help should be sought (see Chapter 10).

Gender difference in the grieving process

The aspect of gender differences in the grieving process does not always receive the attention it deserves. More recent research on traumatic grief shows the necessity of taking into consideration these differences. Women are at twice as much risk for post-traumatic stress as men, even when both genders are exposed to the same events. A number of studies have also shown that women report more intense and persistent grief reactions than men. Women also have a tendency to use confrontation strategies in coping with their loss. This means that they want to talk about and share feelings about what happens. Co-rumination or brooding is therefore a larger problem for women than for men.[11]

Men more frequently employ avoidance strategies, which means that they try to refrain from thinking about or addressing the death to a greater extent than women. A number of men use activity or work to distance themselves from the death. Men are also more likely to use activities and rituals to cope with their experiences or express their feelings by connecting a story to what happened. In this way, feelings acquire a slightly less personal and more distanced quality. Men also have a larger and clearer focus on moving on in life and some have such a strong focus on this that they avoid 'lingering' over their grief.

With an eye towards the significance of being able to oscillate between proximity to and distance from a loss, as in the dual process model, men and women have a lot to learn from one another. In general, men can teach women to distance themselves a bit more and to work at moving on in life, while men can learn from women's ability to approach and tolerate being present in their pain.

Grief is energy-consuming

The grief following a suicide is extremely energy-consuming for the bereaved for many reasons. These include lack of sleep, reduced intake of food and vitamins, recurring ruminations and questions about why the suicide occurred. In addition, one must address the shock and emotional internal chaos, organize all the practical matters and relate to the people around one. At the same time, one has to attempt to move on in life. A mother describes the suicide of her teenage son and reflects upon the grief process and reorientation as follows:

> When something like this happens, it's a shock. You…you lose your footing. You hit bottom. And you have to slowly build yourself up again. For me, I felt as if my heart had been torn in two and he had taken one of the halves with him. So I am left with half a heart to share with the others. I have my daughter, I have my husband and I have my job to share it with. I have myself – who I am supposed to build up again. I have my home and at the same time I am supposed to let the grief come and be allowed to show it. And we are to take care of friends. You hit bottom and you are supposed to be slowly built up again. Where do you start? You have to start carefully. You can't just go right back to work and use up all of your energy there. Because it takes so much energy to build oneself up again.

Grief takes time

Norwegian research on parents who are now in the second decade after a child's death shows that grief is long-term.[12] The grief is usually at its most intense and exhausting at the beginning, and most experience that it changes character throughout the course of the year after the death. Many find, however, that it intensifies on significant days or holidays, or when something brings the loss back to the surface again.[13] Nevertheless, it becomes almost imperceptibly easier after a while. First, a few brighter hours or a bright day will emerge now and then out of the darkness; then gradually the death recedes more into the distance and the good memories emerge more frequently and with greater clarity. This is the description of a mother who lost her young son:

> Two and a half years have passed now since Stephen died and not a day passes that he is not in my thoughts. The difference now is that I can also think about him with joy, in spite of the grief and feelings of loss.

For the bereaved who react with great intensity and for a long time, ideas that grief has a set beginning and defined end point can create problems. The people around them often have a time-frame in mind, according to which they expect that the situation will have improved once the first months after the death have passed. They will then often hope to hear an uplifting reply when they ask how things are going. The pressure to answer 'Things are going fine' or 'I'm doing better now' is great. Very often the network underestimates how much time it takes before those bereaved by suicide begin to see the light at the end of the tunnel. Some aspects of grief will continue for the rest of their lives.

LIFE CRISIS AND REORIENTATION

As discussed previously, suicide is both a trauma and a loss for close loved ones. Many bereaved people experience that 'the world is turned upside down' and that 'everything safe has now become unsafe', that life is experienced as being extremely unfair and that one does not have control. The bereaved can experience such reactions for a long time after the loss. Much that we take for granted in daily life no longer applies, and the brutal upheaval imposes enormous demands with respect to adjusting to what has happened, at both the intellectual and emotional level.[14]

A father who lost his young son writes about how the suicide shook up all of his basic assumptions and how he had to orientate himself to rediscover his footing in life:

Life can be compared with a journey through a city. The journey begins on the one side of the city – and when you have reached the other side, the journey is over. To start with you fumble a bit, go back and forth on the side streets until you find the main street. A more or less goal-oriented journey begins. The streets are paved, there are regulated crossings. Traffic lights ensure that the journey will be safe. As you gradually come closer and closer to the downtown area, the conditions get better and better and you are sure that you are on the right track.

But *all of a sudden* there is a red light – stop. This is no longer your main street. You have to turn right and drive on the street running parallel to this street. When you eventually turn on to your new main street, everything is no longer clear. It is early morning for those who live in the city, so that you can't see very much of your new street. Is it long or short? Is it paved? Are there turns and potholes? Are there street lights and regulated intersections?

Suddenly there is a lot that you do not know about the journey to the other side of the city…

The above testimony illustrates how a suicide turns the life of the bereaved upside down and creates chaos, because the world suddenly becomes unpredictable, uncertain and unsafe. This is a chaos that is not only a disorderly existence, but a chaos that is also related to the loss of other people.[15] The 'rules of the road' that one previously took for granted no longer function, and old patterns of thinking, feeling and action must be revised in order to be able to function in daily life. This imposes great demands on one's thoughts, emotions and social activities. Almost two years after the above testimony was written, the same father explains how far he has come in his reorientation:

If we are going to put this into a time-frame, then I would say that we have driven down the first block of the new street. We are beginning to get an idea about our new street. We are beginning to sense the outline of the new street in our journey through life. It's beginning to fall a bit into place.

In the midst of a life crisis and grief, most bereaved people have thoughts and reflections that leave permanent traces in the form of personal and social changes. Many bereaved people will review the suicide, what happened and why, and their own responsibility (self-reproach) over and over again. While during the early period after a suicide the bereaved often look for an explanation for why the death occurred, later many are concerned about seeking or creating new meaning in life and integrating the death further into their lives. Those who manage this also manage best over time and create possibilities for personal growth and development.

PERSONAL GROWTH AND DEVELOPMENT

To a certain extent, we create our own reality through the way in which we experience our surroundings and how we organize our thoughts.[16] This makes it possible also to redefine reality and create new meaning. Growth in the aftermath of crises such as suicide is an example of such redefinition through reorientation and the creation of a new system of meaning.

What is post-traumatic growth?

Such personal growth and maturation is often called post-traumatic growth.[17] The bereaved describe this as the experiencing of obtaining:

- new possibilities in life

- better/closer relations to others

- increased personal strength

- increased appreciation of life

- enhanced religious or spiritual development.

In addition, one often finds that the bereaved want to and find meaning in being able to help others in the same situation, or they want to work towards prevention, so that others will be spared the experience of bereavement by suicide.

Research shows that most adults and young people who go through a serious crisis experience personal growth in the longer term. While findings from international research indicate that a full 75–90 per cent go through such positive personal changes after a traumatic loss, this was the case for 85 per cent in two Norwegian studies of those bereaved by suicide.[18] For all of the changes described, some bereaved people will experience all of them, while others experience some or none at all.

The following quotations from Norwegians bereaved by suicide illuminate different aspects of post-traumatic growth:

> I find that as a result of what unfortunately happened I have become a stronger person.
>
> I don't bother about trivialities any longer. Now I know what is important and what is not important.
>
> When we buy something new, furniture or something like that, I feel like it's nice to have it. But I don't feel any joy about it, because it is material things. I derive much more joy from other people and children.
>
> Material goods mean less to me and many 'problems' in society have become luxury problems.

I will never be the same person I was before the death. It was the beginning of a new era. My scale of values has completely changed. That which had great value before, and you appreciated very much, is now nothing. It is therefore so absurd sometimes when I watch discussion programmes on TV. They use phrases such as 'enormous tragedy' and it is nothing. At work I hear colleagues sitting and talking about private problems and it is nothing. Then I prefer to leave the situation or go out. My scale of values has been turned upside down.

Life has acquired a deeper meaning, not so superficial. Small things give me greater joy.

Take care of the moment, tomorrow it may be too late!

The desire to help others

Many bereaved people find it meaningful to work towards making the death, once it is a reality, something that can contribute to helping others. They become active in different ways so that something meaningful can come out of what is meaningless. This provides an experience that the person who took his or her own life did not die wholly in vain, if somebody can be helped through his or her death. Many bereaved people may agree to participate in research projects or want to support others who have lost somebody close. They take part in bereavement groups, associations for those who have suffered the same type of loss or meet with others, such as couples, or one to one, as discussed in Chapter 9. This manner of coping and finding meaning has an extroverted, social form and has been a great source of help for many bereaved people.

Intimacy and friendship acquire greater significance

There is another and more private form of creating meaning that is more related to the family unit. Here, the bereaved draw attention to how the death has taught them to appreciate their loved ones in a more heartfelt manner. In retrospect, the bereaved often say that they feel richer than before the death and that this richness in relationships is more important than any material wealth. The people one loves are not taken for granted because one knows how short the distance is between life and death. The creation of meaning in this sense involves giving greater priority to close human relations rather than material objects. There is a great emphasis on unity in the family and intimacy and friendship. Many appreciate the family more than before and want to dedicate more time and attention to those they are closest to, rather than peripheral acquaintances. The bereaved describe the significance of showing the people one loves that one does so, both in words and through physical closeness. Because in their new situation the bereaved require something more and deeper in their relations with others, some of the people who were their friends before the death can be replaced if after the death the relationship is experienced as empty and the conversations too shallow. However, the bereaved more frequently experience that what has happened has brought them closer to other family members or that ties with friends and fellow human beings have become stronger. Many bereaved people find that it is more important than before to take care of one another and of life and to overlook trivialities. Some emphasize this creation of meaning as a change in their priorities and values, while others experience that they have become less superficial because they have now changed their 'life philosophy'. A bereaved father says: 'The relation between people and particularly those who are close becomes important. Material and everyday things become less essential.'

Maturity, personal insight and self-confidence

Another way of creating meaning is found in those who emphasize the personal maturation they have experienced. Many speak of how they have more contact with their own feelings than previously. Others maintain that they have learned to put their thoughts and reactions into words – here it is perhaps men who develop the most. Some feel more self-confident and can say that they no longer simply accept what others do to them; they know how to speak up if they are treated unfairly at work, for example. This personal maturation can also have another dimension, in that the bereaved express that through their own difficulties they have acquired greater understanding and empathy for others' problems. They understand better what others in a crisis need and that they now will be far more courageous and direct in relation to other bereaved people. The Bereavement Project showed that the bereaved also help others in difficult situations more frequently than they did before the death, as was the case for this woman: 'I have gained another understanding of what is important, I set different priorities. I am more sensitive to other people's grief and try to do more for others.'

Seize the day!

Finding meaning also takes the form of a greater sense of gratitude for living, arising from the fact that one sees life from another perspective, that one finds it is possible to enjoy life more, that one appreciates more the small things in daily life and that life is lived fully every day. Death has become more immediate for many and one is aware that the distance between life and death is shorter than one previously thought. For some, this leads to making fewer plans and taking things as they come to a greater extent than before. Some bereaved people say that it becomes more intense to be a human being and that the death contributes to their living life more fully because they recognize that it can come to an end very quickly. Seizing the day also applies in relation to other people, as was the case for a bereaved mother who learned to live by the following rule: 'As human beings we should not take one another for granted. Nobody knows what tomorrow will bring. Take care of one another today.'

GROWTH – A DIFFICULT CONCEPT FOR THE BEREAVED

The intention here is not to imply that life becomes a bowl of cherries after one has suddenly lost someone beloved. That is not how it is. On the contrary, such positive life changes, when they occur, do so against a backdrop of pain, longing and feelings of loss. It is therefore important to emphasize that the concept of growth refers to the experience of positive changes in the aftermath of a substantial loss. Nonetheless, it is difficult for many bereaved people to acknowledge and put into words that something positive has come out of the tragedy of losing somebody by suicide. There are therefore very few bereaved who speak about such personal growth, at least not until long after the death. And if the topic should come up, the bereaved stress that they would have preferred to have been without this growth and instead have the deceased with them.

We think that it is nonetheless important to consider post-traumatic growth, in order that the bereaved will understand how common and normal it is, to enable an understanding of why it happens and perhaps to contribute to removing the guilty conscience of some over the fact that something positive can come out of something as tragic as a suicide.

Personal growth and mental health

It is important to emphasize that personal growth entails change in relation to how the individual was before his or her loss and therefore is not the same as coping. It is possible to have good coping abilities without experiencing the changes that are described here. But those who manage to use active coping strategies combined with the ability for reorientation often experience more growth. There is also evidence indicating that bereaved people who experience the greatest amount of growth are also those who relate to the loss and grief by oscillating between re-experiencing and avoidance of memories about the death to a larger extent than those who experience less growth.

The explanation for this is that such individuals also succeed in distancing to a sufficient degree and in implementing denial strategies as a means of keeping that which is most painful at a distance when necessary or constructive. Research shows that those who experience the greatest growth also have fewer ailments and difficulties after the death than those who experience less growth. Those who experience personal growth are, for example, less troubled by depression and have a better quality of life and well-being than those who experience less growth. Most studies also establish that the greater the amount of time that has passed since the traumatic event, the greater the connection found between personal growth and mental health.[19]

How to achieve personal growth?

Many bereaved people gradually recognize that their state of mind for the rest of their lives depends on how they manage to interject meaning into something that is apparently meaningless. The creation of meaning that the individual is able to carry out will have an impact on the quality of life and growth that they experience personally and together with their family and social networks. For many bereaved people, the processes leading to growth entail managing to pull oneself up by one's bootstraps and actively work against falling apart, as this women who lost her young son admitted: 'It is important to grow in one's grief and not to fall apart with it.'

Although understanding about the connections between post-traumatic growth and health is increasing, it is impossible to provide a recipe for the achievement of such positive changes. Bereaved individuals differ far too much for this. What is good for one is not necessarily good for another. Each individual must find his or her own way. Nonetheless, there are some rules of thumb that will apply for most:

- Confront the pain and loss – while at the same time protecting and distancing yourself from the pain from time to time (as addressed earlier in this chapter).

- Force yourself to take a time out from problems, thoughts and ruminations now and then (as discussed in Chapter 7).

- Implement different coping strategies that suit you, do things you liked to do before the death (as addressed in Chapter 7).

- Spend time with and accept support from your network – don't isolate yourself (as discussed in Chapter 8).

- Accept support from other bereaved people if this is available and you wish for it (as discussed in Chapter 9).

- Accept or ask for help from professionals if necessary – either to confront or distance yourself from the death and loss (as discussed in Chapter 10).

Can professionals contribute to personal growth on the part of the bereaved?

Because personal growth is experienced as 'inappropriate' for many bereaved people, it is not always the case that such subjects are brought up by therapists or other helpers after a suicide. It is therefore important for professionals to be aware that such growth often occurs with time. They can then provide opportunities for discussions about positive changes and view these as resources for the grieving process and continued life of the bereaved.

Research has shown that those who do not experience growth and change struggle to a greater extent with depression and receive less helpful support from their social network. Their ability to keep things at a distance is also weaker than among those who do experience post-traumatic growth. Professionals can use such knowledge to promote personal growth.[20]

Professionals must not, however, present post-traumatic growth and development as something positive further down the road, which will come about only if the bereaved are able to do this or that. This can be experienced as hurtful. Professionals should instead call attention to the positive signs of change and growth that they observe and signal to the bereaved that they are on the right track.

CHAPTER 12

Why Suicide?

Life crises that appear very similar can end in death for some, while others get through them without having had a single thought about ending their lives. Some suicides seem to be wholly incomprehensible, while others are clearly related to mental illness. The latter makes it easier to understand suicide, but nonetheless not completely, because the mentally ill person need not have given any signs that he or she was feeling suicidal. In any case, suicide is an appalling experience for the bereaved and many struggle for a long time with unanswered questions and feelings of guilt.

We cannot expect to find complete answers for all of the difficult questions that the bereaved may struggle with. How could he have done this to us? Why didn't she say anything? Why didn't he leave a note? Why didn't he seek help? Why didn't the therapist do more? What have I done wrong? Why didn't I understand the warning signs? Such questions can seldom be clarified by a simple answer, such as the deceased had lost his or her job, had a mental disorder, was going through a divorce or had conflicts with family or friends.

We know that people can live for years with a mental disorder without killing themselves and that most people manage to handle losing their job or a divorce without becoming suicidal. Others have never shown signs of a serious mental disorder or had serious conflicts with somebody when their life is suddenly ended by suicide. They have, on the contrary, appeared to be exceptionally resourceful and successful. What happens when people do not manage to get through that which they in all likelihood experience as a painful life crisis and where the 'solution' becomes to end their life?

CAN SUICIDE BE EXPLAINED?

The purpose of this chapter is not to give a comprehensive overview of all of the different theoretical approaches found in studies of suicide, but rather to present some elements of the knowledge accumulated about suicidal behaviour that can perhaps give the bereaved an understanding that they can live with. Suicide and suicide attempts are the result of many contributing factors, and each suicide must be understood as the final stage in the development of an extremely unfortunate interaction between both internal and external circumstances. The process may have been ongoing for a long period of time without anyone thinking that the problems would lead to suicide. For others, suicide can happen after a seemingly short-term crisis.

For both the bereaved and professionals, an evaluation of the risk of suicide is difficult, particularly when the strains are apparently no greater than those that the majority of us experience and are able to resolve. In other cases, both the next of kin and therapists have feared suicide over a long period of time. Nonetheless, a suicide can occur at a time when one believed that the risk was not great. Sometimes after a suicide, it is found that insufficient protective measures were taken by treatment institutions, and the thought that those who should have known best did not protect a suicidal person can be an especially heavy burden to bear. It is also a great source of strain if it turns out that a proper assessment of the risk of suicide had not been carried out or if discharge from a mental hospital was unjustifiable. It was such events that led to the Norwegian health authorities in 2007 publishing national guidelines for the prevention of suicide in mental health care.

When one attempts to explain suicide by referring to the fact that the deceased had or must have had a mental illness, lost his or her job, was in the midst of a divorce or something along these lines, this is nonetheless only part of the explanation, although it can be an important part. For example, the vast majority of people suffering from depression do not kill themselves. Lifetime risk for suicide among individuals with a diagnosis of major depression is on average 5 per cent.[1] The risk is greater if the depression resulted in admission to a mental hospital. Accordingly, the majority of those who suffer from serious depression do not take their own lives. This means that there are other factors in addition to the depression itself, and not the depression alone, which can explain an individual suicide. Lifetime risk of suicide in connection with schizophrenia is approximately the same.[2] There is therefore no doubt that having a serious mental illness increases the risk of both suicide attempts and suicide, but to understand an individual suicide one must include all of the factors that have contributed to making life intolerably painful. The same holds for stressful, negative life events. It is, for example, unusual to take one's life due to unemployment alone, and although ruptures in close relationships can precede a suicidal act, only a minority actually take their lives in such situations. Serious childhood traumas, such as physical, psychological or sexual abuse, can lead to suicide but most will survive, even with serious psychological problems. For the bereaved, it is important to know that suicide is bound up with an accumulation of factors, even if an isolated painful incident can be the final straw.

SUICIDOLOGY

Suicidology (teachings about the different aspects of suicide and suicide attempts) is an interdisciplinary science, made up of knowledge from a range of fields. Suicidology can therefore appear to be excessively complex and hard to understand. Because different parts of suicidology play different roles in the understanding of an individual suicide, more than one way of illuminating and providing an understanding is necessary. We will most likely think differently about a serious suicide attempt by a person recently diagnosed with schizophrenia, as opposed to a moderate overdose of harmless pills on the part of an ordinary teenager with a broken heart. Nonetheless, there are common features found in the act itself: faced with what is experienced as a serious life crisis, there are those who give up where others will fight their way through it. Below we present some different ways of understanding suicide which we hope will be helpful for the bereaved in their endeavours to understand. In the last decade, suicidology has undergone great development, and much new knowledge means that we are increasingly better equipped to understand when a suicidal crisis is on a dangerous course, so that we can prevent suicide to a greater extent.[3]

DIFFERENT WAYS OF UNDERSTANDING SUICIDE

Suicidology comprises the sum total of different professional approaches and is characterized by competing — in part — theories of knowledge. Suicidology is not alone in this sense, but the consequences of an inadequate professional understanding of suicidal crises can be dramatically different for suicidal individuals and their closely related than for people experiencing other types of life crisis. For the bereaved, it can be difficult to receive a type of explanation that does not correspond with their personal experience of why things went so wrong and which is perhaps based on only one of a number of possible perspectives. Both in Norway and elsewhere in the Western world, it is the illness model that has up to now had the greatest impact on how suicide has been explained and understood.

On the basis of the illness model, suicide and suicide attempts are defined as symptoms of mental illness. Both prevention and treatment are primarily focused on the underlying illness: primarily, major depression, schizophrenia, personality disorders and substance abuse. Fortunately, the majority of those who suffer from mental illnesses will not take their own lives. For those who do, we try to understand which additional strains contributed to making life intolerable for the individual in question. For some, suicide is directly related to illness, such as with a psychosis in which an internal voice tells you that you have no right to live and must kill yourself, or with a paranoid psychotic state in which you are convinced that you are being followed by somebody who is really out to destroy you. For most, however, it is the combined accumulation of internal psychological pressure and external events that leads to suicidal acts. Both internationally and in Norway, better treatment of suicidal patients in mental health care is a primary area of investment, and to an increasing extent there is an emphasis on understanding suicide at both the individual and system level. However, the very complexity of suicidal crises in itself will make it difficult to find one specific treatment method that is suitable for everyone, even though there are some common features to take as a starting point.[4] Changing the treatment culture in many of the institutions within mental health care in ways that make it possible to implement research-based treatment methods remains fraught with great challenges.

INTERACTION OF FACTORS

In the course of the past few decades, the professional approach to suicidal behaviour has to an increasingly greater extent shifted from being purely illness-based to a more interaction-oriented understanding, in that external life conditions are included. Different psychological theories of suicide and suicidal behaviour have been developed; many of them have led to specific treatment protocols. Each theory, while emphasizing the critical role of the individual's intrapsychic experience, also recognizes the importance of social context.[5]

On the basis of an interaction model, suicide is viewed as a reaction to problems that have developed between the individual and their significant others over a (short or long) period of time. Significant others may imply everybody from the immediate family to therapists, friends, colleagues, classmates and others important for the individual's quality of life. In the context of such a process, the risk of suicide can vary in intensity and can change from being virtually absent to intense in the course of a short period of time. Such fluctuations can be related to ordinary life experiences, particularly related to people of importance to the person in question, or an individual can be overwhelmed by negative thoughts without any obvious triggering incident. It is, for example, worse to be in a serious conflict with people who are close to you than with people who are not a part of one's closest circle. It can also be worse handling humiliation at work if one's career is the most important channel for self-esteem than if one's job has a more subordinate position in one's life. Being discharged from a treatment facility when you are afraid that your suicidal impulses may get out of control can also trigger suicidal behaviour. Being bullied over a long period of time without seeing any solution can also break down a person's self-esteem and lead to suicidal acts. In other words, people are more vulnerable or less vulnerable to negative life events, and this vulnerability plays a key part in the interaction-based understanding of suicide. Professionals have not always been sufficiently attentive to the interaction between factors which, taken individually, would not be sufficient as an explanation for suicide, but which in combination can acquire lethal force. Below we consider some factors that different researchers and clinicians have focused on.

VULNERABILITY–STRESS UNDERSTANDING OF SUICIDALITY

Many different theories of knowledge about suicide correspond with a vulnerability–stress model, such as the model by Schotte and Clum,[6] which provides the foundation for most subsequent models. In these models, suicidality is related to an understanding of individual vulnerability in interaction with the surroundings. In purely logical terms, suicide can be a comprehensible act on the part of an individual who in the midst of a life crisis sees no other solution.[7]

The vulnerability of an individual can be related to biological, psychiatric, psychological and/or social factors. Personality traits that appear to be requisite conditions for a suicide attempt include poor impulse control, a tendency to think in black and white, low self-esteem and little faith in the individual's own ability to cope with future crises, even when he or she may have mastered many previous crises and from the outside appear to be managing well in many difficult situations. Particularly vulnerable people are those in the midst of interpersonal conflicts where the threat of a rupture or an actual rupture in close relations is a contributing factor in connection with a suicidal crisis.[8]

Some suicides occur specifically as a result of a conflict with someone who was close to the deceased, and studies of notes to the bereaved illustrate resignation in the face of conflicts that appear to have no solution, such as in connection with a break-up with a partner. After a suicide, most bereaved will be interested in learning whether the deceased was in the midst of such difficult conflicts in relation to other people. Some bereaved will blame themselves for having been in conflict with the person who took his or her own life, and assume an unreasonable amount of responsibility for causing it. In other suicide notes to the bereaved, the deceased can express that he or she was afraid that the people around him or her would one day see what was behind the facade and that the image of the deceased as successful would then be shattered. But the choice of suicide is contingent upon far more than an individual situation of conflict. We will therefore consider some common features which a number of professionals view as important in relation to both suicide and suicide attempts.

Suicide can be understood as a desperate attempt to get out of what is experienced as a situation of irresolvable conflict

This implies that suicide is viewed there and then as the only solution for that which the individual is experiencing as an unendurable life crisis.[9] The suicide is experienced as being the only guarantee that the situation will not get even worse, because the individual feels trapped inside a painful situation that seems irresolvable and feels that it is impossible to find his or her way out of in any other way.[10] In order to understand suicide in retrospect, one must attempt to see the total number of pressures, while at the same time ignoring one's own assessment of the problems and trying to understand what the deceased may have been going through. As a rule, suicide is not a random act but is rather related to the combination of vulnerability and the individual's experienced problems, even if the act can seem impulsive. In hindsight, it is often the case that the problems do not appear irresolvable for the bereaved, but the problems there and then must have appeared so for the person who gave up.

Suicide is related to the need to bring an end to suffering and stop disturbing thoughts

Sometimes the point of suicide is to take a break – not necessarily to die. This is likely to be the case for more impulsive suicides. Intolerable thoughts and feelings can be related to psychotic conditions, but can also arise in individuals under great internal and external pressure, without this being related to a psychotic condition. For some people, their vulnerability to conflicts or difficulties is greater than for others, so it is always important to view each suicide in light of the individual person's vulnerability. Although a suicide can appear to be incomprehensible for most people, the internal pressure nonetheless can have been enormous and the psychological pressure there and then unbearable. The understanding of a suicide must therefore be based on the life history of the individual as well as the triggering crisis.[11]

Most suicides are related to a feeling of intolerable psychological pain

It is the elimination of the pain of living that is wished for. We emphasize that it is the individual's subjectively experienced pain that is the force behind the suicidal act, not our assessment of it. It is not always the case that those around the suicidal individual are able to see that life feels extremely heavy and painful if the person who is suffering does not express this. And still it is the case that men to a greater degree than women refrain from seeking help for psychological problems, so that it can be particularly difficult for those around them to know how painful life may be for them. A suicidal crisis will of course entail many interwoven feelings, such as anger, hate, shame, guilt, fear, protest or longing for a beloved person who has passed away. Many believe that it is the common denominator of all of these feelings – in other words, the pain of feeling this way and the lack of will or ability to tolerate this pain – that contributes to suicidal behaviour.[12]

Key feelings of the psychological pain are helplessness and hopelessness

More or less clearly, the suicidal individual may have thought, 'There is nothing I can do (except take my own life), and there is nobody who can help me (with the pain I am tormented by).' In the midst of the various thoughts and feelings, hopelessness and helplessness are the strongest triggers of suicidal acts. There is a broad professional consensus that it is the aspect of hopelessness in depression that can potentially lead to suicide.[13] For individuals who live with great psychological pain, the suicide can be experienced as a logical reaction to experiences connected to loss and rejection. The hope of another solution to the experienced psychological existential pain must be extinguished when the decision to take one's life is made.

For some, a key impetus behind suicidal behaviour will be long-term frustration about fundamental psychological needs that are not met

Human behaviour is influenced by a number of psychological needs which in different ways we seek to have met. Most suicidal acts occur in frustration about what the person in question experiences as a lack in connection with one or more of these needs – for example, belonging, security, care, love, respect, acceptance and challenge. Many of those who have attempted to take their lives by suicide state that they have lived with such feelings for a long time and, for some, such fundamental needs have never been met. Nonetheless, they may have demonstrated a facade that functioned relatively well, and for some it can be on the day that the facade breaks down that life becomes unbearable because of a feeling of being left without self-worth. Some suicide notes have contents that reflect such a process of personal devaluation, which will be an additional burden for the next of kin. Most suicide notes however, contain another message, namely that the deceased blames nobody but him/herself. It is the individual's own limitations that have prevented him or her from having satisfactory relationships with other people. In this context, we would like to emphasize how important it is for the bereaved to process their own reactions in such cases, to help prevent the development of a suicidal crisis of their own. Different therapeutic models for treatment of suicidal risk have been developed, and in Norway and in other countries work is being done on developing the best possible (evidence-based) therapy forms for different sub-groups of suicidal individuals, in which the focus of treatment is more on the risk of suicide than on the assumed or diagnosed fundamental disorder.[14]

Suicidal acts are usually associated with ambivalence – the individual both wanted and did not want to end his or her life

Many bereaved people struggle to understand why the deceased both said and did things which clearly expressed that he or she had plans for the future, even right before the suicide. This can be connected with the phenomenon of ambivalence, meaning that one can have conflicting feelings and thoughts at the same time. This implies that we must not perceive a suicide attempt as less serious if the individual who made the attempt also calls for help and is saved as a result. It is more the rule rather than the exception that individuals at risk of suicide demonstrate such contradictory behaviour.

We know from suicide notes and the stories of people who have survived against all odds that even doing something which will almost guarantee death has not always been a choice wished for with 100 per cent certainty. For the bereaved, this point can offer understanding about the fact that a suicide occurred even though the deceased, just a short period before taking his or her own life, expressed that he or she was against suicide as a solution and would not do such a thing personally. The ambivalence can fluctuate rapidly between wanting and not wanting to end one's life, and in response to direct questions, the deceased may there and then have thought and felt that he or she would not do such a thing. Immediately thereafter, the ambivalence can swing over to the dark thoughts and the desire to live can disappear long enough to make the suicide a fact.

Thoughts and feelings in connection with the risk of suicide are typically constricted (tunnel vision)

So-called tunnel vision entails a more or less transitory constriction of both feelings and thoughts. This means that the danger of suicide involves a gradual narrowing of alternative solutions to a life crisis as desperation increases. This narrowing of alternative courses of action also entails that the common consideration humans have for their next of kin slides out of focus and loses its normal power to control one's actions. In this process, the risk of suicide increases as the person's thinking becomes more black and white, in that he or she does not see any middle solutions between death and a complete end to all problems. For some, this change in one's normal reactionary patterns is frightening, and for some it triggers an anxiety about becoming or being insane. For others, the process can entail an erroneous perception of themselves as a burden and that next of kin are thus better off without them in the long run. In the context of such a perspective, the decision to end their life seems both considerate and logical.[15]

All suicidal acts contain an element of escape

To abandon life by suicide entails an unambiguous message of escape from everything that is painful in life. For some bereaved people, it seems cowardly to run away in this manner; others can perceive suicide as a courageous act. If death by suicide is evaluated as an expression of strength, the suicide can paradoxically be a means of enhancing one's self-esteem. Running away from life's problems is hardly an easy act and must be seen in light of the other elements that we have explained here. In a painful process, there are some who feel that the only remaining option is to escape, and it is neither cowardly nor brave, but rather the result of a constricted cognitive function and resignation. In a suicidal crisis, the threshold for suicidal acts can be lowered if one has easy access to the means, such as medication or a firearm.

Most people at risk of suicide warn those around them of their plan before they carry it out

This point contrasts sharply with the experience of many that a good number of suicides occur without warning. There is a consensus of opinion among professionals that some type of warning is given in approximately 80 per cent of all suicides. However, a large problem is that some of these warnings are disguised and unclear and cannot be unequivocally interpreted as suicidal messages other than through the illumination of hindsight. People who plan a suicide will, because most are ambivalent, consciously or unconsciously send out signals that they are having a very difficult time, feel helpless, feel that everything is hopeless, are planning to move away, can't take any more and so on. Some speak openly about the fact that they are having suicidal thoughts, thinking that speaking about such thoughts serves as protection from the act itself. Those around them can also believe that speaking about suicidal thoughts serves as protection against suicide.

Here we are shaking up the myth that if somebody speaks about ending their life by suicide, he or she won't carry it out. It is, on the contrary, actually the case that having thoughts or plans of taking one's life puts people in the risk group for suicide.[16] The fact that many studies show that warning is given in up to 80 per cent of all suicides, without people around them in all cases picking up on this, indicates that both the public health services and next of kin can easily come to blame themselves for not understanding that suicide was imminent. We must recognize that some suicides occur without warning and that other suicides occur following a type of warning that is so indirect and camouflaged that it was not possible for those around them to understand what the warning was actually about. In addition to this, suicide is such an extreme action that we nonetheless have difficulty fully comprehending that it is in fact close at hand.

Cognitive function – how we think

Outlining how the deceased handled previous life crises can shed light upon some suicides. As a rule, it is possible to discern a relatively fixed pattern in people's coping strategies throughout life; it is not the case that we change dramatically in different life phases or in relation to different life events. Some people have a low tolerance for problems in general, low tolerance for psychological pressure, high expectations with regard to succeeding in all areas of life, or problems managing the large and small challenges of daily life. With recurring or chronic mental illness, the belief in one's own ability to cope over time can be seriously debilitated. A number of the therapeutic methods that now appear to be effective in the prevention of suicide are focused on such inexpedient cognitive and emotional 'short circuits'.[17]

THE ACCUMULATION OF DIFFERENT TYPES OF STRAIN

Suicidal acts are connected to a total accumulation of pressures, and that which may appear to be a trivial triggering event must be viewed in light of psychological pressure that may have accumulated gradually. The deceased may in the end have felt trapped in a situation from which there did not appear to be any way out. Because each suicide is unique, it is not easy to provide a key to understanding that is suitable for all cases. The suicides that are the simplest to explain are perhaps those related to psychotic episodes; some of the most difficult are related to those people who function well (often men) and who apparently appear to manage everything until the day they crack. For the bereaved, our advice is that one should attempt to see the totality of possible contributing factors and not take on unnecessary feelings of guilt – for example, by putting too much importance on a particular comment or a less significant incident. For some bereaved people, professionals can be of great significance with respect to promoting such an understanding.

SUICIDE-RELATED LIFE CRISES

One way to understand suicide can be that the individual experiences being trapped in a life situation that seems hopeless in relation to the possibilities that each individual feels he or she has to change significant aspects of the situation.[18] Existence feels intolerable and the perspective of the future contains no good solutions. The feeling of hopelessness in connection with a self-assessment of the limited possibilities available to realize the life one dreams of and has expectations in relation to appears to be a contributing factor for some. But suicide can also occur after many years of mental illness, in which the individual who is ill gives up all hope of returning to the life he or she desires. Similar thoughts about an irresolvable life situation can develop on the part of people who do not suffer from a serious mental disorder, particularly when one feels there is a grave discrepancy between the requirements one has for oneself in order to feel worthwhile and one's achievements. We all know that a fragile self-esteem can hide behind a seemingly competent facade. Not seeking help from others when one has such thoughts contributes to creating an internal pressure which with time can lead to suicide.

THERAPY IN CONNECTION WITH THE RISK OF SUICIDE

In terms of content, no one specific form of therapy for the risk of suicide has been developed, but several types of cognitive therapy (with a focus on cognitive 'short circuits') have shown promising results. There is an international consensus with respect to the necessity of developing better treatment for individuals at risk of suicide, with a specific focus on that which leads to suicidal behaviour and beyond the traditional treatment of mental illness.[19] Research findings show that many make contact with the public health services during the final weeks before the suicide, without the risk of suicide being adequately identified, which underlines the need for increased knowledge about suicide among general practitioners and other health professionals.

THE MAIN MESSAGE

We hope that this book can assist in helping to put the bereaved on the right path in terms of finding some answers to the question of why the life of their loved one ended with suicide. Some may not find anything that fits with their story or that of their client. That is how it will be. Although we know a number of the common features of suicide, an individual suicide will always contain personal experiences, thoughts and feelings which perhaps nobody else knew about because they were not communicated to anyone.

The main message is nonetheless that suicide is the final destination in a fatal interaction between internal forces and external events, and there is seldom one single event which can explain it. We will always have limited possibilities for putting ourselves into the thoughts and feelings of another human being, and we must make a distinction between what we believe the thoughts of the deceased to have been and what they in fact were. Many bereaved people must therefore also live with unanswered questions.

Useful Resources

INTERNATIONAL WEBSITE LINKS

Many countries have websites for suicide/the bereaved by suicide. Below is a selection of links:

International Befrienders Worldwide: www.befrienders.org/support/helplines.asp

Australia Lifeline Australia – Suicide Bereavement (postvention): www.lifeline.org.au
The Australian Child and Adolescent Trauma, Loss and Grief Network: www.carlytraumagricf.anu.edu.au/resource_hubs/early_childhood_schools_hub/suicide_postvention

Canada Canadian Association for Suicide Prevention – Support groups across Canada: www.suicideprevention.ca

Denmark Landsforeningen for efterladte efter selvmord (National Association for the Survivors of Suicide): www.efterladte.dk

Germany Angehörige um Suizid (AGUS) (Relatives of Suicide): www.agus-selbsthilfe.de

Ireland National Suicide Bereavement Support Network: www.nsbsn.org

Norway Landsforeningen for etterlatte ved selvmord (LEVE) (The Norwegian Organization for Suicide Survivors) www.levenorge.no

Sweden Suicid Prevention och Efterlevandes Stöd (SPES) (National Association for Suicide Prevention and Survivor Support): www.spes.nu

UK Survivors of Bereavement by Suicide: www.uk-sobs.org.uk

USA American Association of Suicidology – Suicide loss survivors: www.suicidology.org/web/guest/suicide-loss-survivors
American Foundation for Suicide Prevention: www.afsp.org
Suicide Prevention Action Network USA (SPAN USA): www.spanusa.org
Suicide Prevention Resource Center: www.sprc.org

RESEARCH PROJECTS REFERRED TO IN THIS BOOK

Reference is made throughout the book to several Norwegian studies carried out by Dr Kari Dyregrov and her research groups. Below, a brief description is given of some of the projects mentioned most frequently. For further information about results, selection and sources of data, see www.krisepsyk.no (mostly in Norwegian).

THE BEREAVEMENT PROJECT (*OMSORGSPROSJEKTET*)

The Bereavement Project investigated how the bereaved experienced and coped with their situation following a suicide, the type of help and support they received and what they had felt a need for in the way of help and support. All families that had lost a child under the age of 30 by suicide in Norway in the period between July 1997 and December 1998 were invited to take part in the project. Of these, 197 parents and siblings filled out the questionnaire and 47 were interviewed. The project was funded by the Norwegian Extra Foundation for Health and Rehabilitation and was terminated in 2000. The project has resulted in a doctoral thesis and many academic articles as well as articles, written for the general public.

THE NETWORK PROJECT (*NETTVERKSPROSJEKTET*)

The Network Project investigated how social networks experienced their support for the bereaved after a sudden death (also suicide), the types of challenges they encountered and how the challenges can be addressed. The members of the Norwegian SIDS and Stillbirth Society (LUB) and The Norwegian Organization for Suicide Survivors (LEVE) were asked to invite friends and family members who had provided support to take part in the research project. A total of 101 friends, neighbours, colleagues, etc. filled out the questionnaire and 21 groups who had supported the bereaved by suicide took part in focus group interviews. The project received financing from the LUB research fund and was terminated in 2005. The project has resulted in a book and a number of scholastic articles, as well as articles written for the general public.

THE PROJECT FOR THE YOUNG BEREAVED BY SUICIDE (*UNGELEVE¬PROSJEKTET*)

The Project for the Young Bereaved by Suicide[1] project investigated how young people bereaved by suicide experienced their situation and the type of needs they had for care. The focus was on the types of experiences young people had with receiving help and support – both from the public help service, the school and their social network. Further, the project investigated whether the young people would have preferred the help to have been different: What type of help/support would they had preferred? Who did they want to receive help from? How would they have preferred to have been met? When is it important to be approached with help? What scope should the help have and for how long should it be available? Which type of quality/expertise had they felt a need for? What would they have liked the contents of the support to be? Recruitment was carried out by way of youth gatherings under the direction of LEVE, and 32 young bereaved filled out the questionnaire and took part in focus group interviews. The Project was financed by the Norwegian Extra Foundation for Health and Rehabilitation and was terminated in 2006.

Endnotes

CHAPTER 2

1. Shneidman, E. (1985) *Definition of Suicide.* New York, NY: Wiley.
2. Lester, D. (2008) 'Suicide and culture.' *World Cultural Psychiatry Research Review 3,* 2, 51–68.
3. Jordan, J.R. and McIntosh, J.L. (eds) (2011) *Grief After Suicide: Understanding the Consequences and Caring for the Survivors.* New York, NY, and London: Routledge.
4. Dyregrov, K. (2011) 'International Perspectives on Suicide Bereavement: Suicide Survivors and Postvention in Norway.' In J.R. Jordan and J.L. McIntosh (eds) *Understanding the Consequences and Caring for the Survivors.* New York, NY: Routledge.

    Wertheimer, A. (2001) *A Special Scar: The Experiences of People Bereaved by Suicide,* 2nd revised edition. London: Taylor & Francis.
5. Kearl, M.C. (1989) *Endings: A Sociology of Death and Dying.* New York, NY: Oxford University Press.
6. Durkheim, E. (1952) *Suicide.* London: Routledge, Kegan & Paul.
7. Dyregrov, K. (2011) 'International Perspectives on Suicide Bereavement: Suicide Survivors and Postvention in Norway.' In J.R. Jordan and J.L. McIntosh (eds) *Understanding the Consequences and Caring for the Survivors.* New York, NY: Routledge.

    Dyregrov, K. (in press) 'What do we know about needs for help after suicide in different parts of the world? A phenomenological perspective.' Available at http://ifp.es.nyu.edu/?p=1205100, accessed 19 July 2011.

    Jordan, J.R. and McIntosh, J.L. (eds) (2011) Grief After Suicide: Understanding the Consequences and Caring for the Survivors. New York, NY, and London: Routledge.
8. Jordan, J.R. and McIntosh, J.L. (eds) (2011) *Grief After Suicide: Understanding the Consequences and Caring for the Survivors.* New York, NY, and London: Routledge.

CHAPTER 4

1. Bonanno, G.A. and Kaltman, S. (2001) 'The varieties of grief experience.' *Clinical Psychology Review 21,* 5, 705–734.
2. Dyregrov, K. and Dyregrov, A. (2008) *Effective Grief and Bereavement Support: The Role of Family, Friends, Colleagues, Schools and Support Professionals.* London: Jessica Kingsley Publishers.
3. Dyregrov, K. and Dyregrov, A. (2008) *Effective Grief and Bereavement Support: The Role of Family, Friends, Colleagues, Schools and Support Professionals.* London: Jessica Kingsley Publishers.
4. Li, J., Precht, D.H., Mortensen, P.B. and Olsen, J. (2003) 'Mortality in parents after death of a child in Denmark: A nationwide follow-up study.' *The Lancet 361,* 9355, 363–367.

CHAPTER 5

1. Goffman, E. (1968) *Stigma: Notes on the Management of Spoiled Identity.* Harmondsworth: Penguin.

    Shneidman, E.S. (1972) 'Foreword.' In A.C. Cain (ed.) *Survivors of Suicide.* Springfield, IL: Charles C. Thomas.

2. Demi, A.S. and Howell, C. (1991) 'Hiding and healing: Resolving the suicide of a parent or sibling.' *Archives of Psychiatric Nursing 5*, 6, 350–6.

3. Dieserud, G. (2000) *Suicide Attempt. Unsolvable Lives?* Doctoral dissertation. Oslo, Norway: Psychological Institute, University of Oslo.

   Ellis, T.E. and Newman, C.F. (1996) *Choosing to Live: How to Defeat Suicide Through Cognitive Therapy*. Oakland, CA: New Harbinger Publications.

   Shneidman, E. (1985) *Definition of Suicide*. New York, NY: Wiley.

   Shneidman, E.S. (1998) *The Suicidal Mind*. Oxford: Oxford University Press.

4. Dyregrov, K. (2003) *The Loss of a Child by Suicide, SIDS, and Accidents: Consequences, Needs and Provisions of Help*. Doctoral dissertation. Bergen, Norway: HEMIL, Faculty of Psychology, University of Bergen.

   Jordan, J.R. and McIntosh, J.L. (eds) (2011) *Grief After Suicide: Understanding the Consequences and Caring for the Survivors*. New York, NY, and London: Routledge.

   Rakic, A.S. (1992) *Sibling Survivors of Adolescent Suicide*. Doctoral dissertation. Alameda, CA: The California School of Professional Psychology, Berkeley/Alameda.

CHAPTER 6

1. Dyregrov, A. (2008) *Grief in Children: A Handbook for Adults*, 2nd edition. London: Jessica Kingsley Publishers.

2. Dyregrov, K. and Dyregrov, A. (2005) 'Siblings after suicide: "The forgotten bereaved".' *Suicide and Life-Threatening Behavior 35*, 6, 714–24.

   Jordan, J.R. and McIntosh, J.L. (eds) (2011) *Grief After Suicide: Understanding the Consequences and Caring for the Survivors*. New York, NY, and London: Routledge. McIntosh, J. and Wrobleski, A. (1988) 'Grief reactions among suicide survivors: An exploratory comparison of relationships.' *Death Studies 12*, 1, 21–39.

3. Dyregrov, K. and Dyregrov, A. (2005) 'Siblings after suicide: "The forgotten bereaved".' *Suicide and Life-Threatening Behavior 35*, 6, 714–24.

   Dyregrov, K. and Dyregrov, A. (2009) 'Helping the Family Following Suicide.' In B. Monroe and F. Kraus (eds) *Brief Interventions with Bereaved Children*, 2nd edition. Oxford: Oxford University Press.

4. Dyregrov, K. and Dyregrov, A. (2005) 'Siblings after suicide: "The forgotten bereaved".' *Suicide and Life-Threatening Behavior 35*, 6, 714–24.

5. Demi, A.S. and Howell, C. (1991) 'Hiding and healing: Resolving the suicide of a parent or sibling.' *Archives of Psychiatric Nursing 5*, 6, 350–6.

   Dyregrov, K. and Dyregrov, A. (2005) 'Siblings after suicide: "The forgotten bereaved".' *Suicide and Life-Threatening Behavior 35*, 6, 714–24.

   Dyregrov, K. and Dyregrov, A. (2009) 'Helping the Family Following Suicide.' In B. Monroe and F. Kraus (eds) *Brief Interventions with Bereaved Children*, 2nd edition. Oxford: Oxford University Press.

6. Dyregrov, K. and Dyregrov, A. (2005) 'Siblings after suicide: "The forgotten bereaved".' *Suicide and Life-Threatening Behavior 35*, 6, 714–24.

   Jordan, J.R. and McIntosh, J.L. (eds) (2011) *Grief After Suicide: Understanding the Consequences and Caring for the Survivors*. New York, NY, and London: Routledge.

   Nelson, B.J. and Frantz, T.T. (1996) 'Family interactions of suicide survivors and survivors of non-suicidal death.' *OMEGA – Journal of Death and Dying 33*, 2, 125–140.

7. Davies, B. (1995) 'Sibling Bereavement Research: State of the Art.' In I.B. Corless, B.B. Germino and M.A. Pittman (eds) *Dying, Death, and Bereavement: A Challenge for Living*. London: Jones and Bartlett Publishers.

   Dyregrov, K. and Dyregrov, A. (2005) 'Siblings after suicide: "The forgotten bereaved".' *Suicide and Life-Threatening Behavior 35*, 6, 714–24.

Dyregrov, K. and Dyregrov, A. (2009) 'Helping the Family Following Suicide.' In B. Monroe and F. Kraus (eds) *Brief Interventions with Bereaved Children,* 2nd edition. Oxford: Oxford University Press.

Jordan, J.R. and McIntosh, J.L. (eds) (2011) *Grief After Suicide: Understanding the Consequences and Caring for the Survivors.* New York, NY, and London: Routledge.

Rakic, A.S. (1992) *Sibling Survivors of Adolescent Suicide.* Doctoral dissertation. Alameda, CA: The California School of Professional Psychology, Berkeley/Alameda.

8. Dyregrov, A. (2008) *Grief in Children: A Handbook for Adults,* 2nd edition. London: Jessica Kingsley Publishers.

    Dyregrov, K. and Dyregrov, A. (2009) 'Helping the Family Following Suicide.' In B. Monroe and F. Kraus (eds) *Brief Interventions with Bereaved Children,* 2nd edition. Oxford: Oxford University Press.

9. Brent, D.A., Perper, J.A., Moritz, G., Liotus, L. *et al.* (1993) 'Psychiatric impact of the loss of an adolescent sibling to suicide.' *Journal of Affective Disorders 28,* 4, 249–56.

    Sethi, S. and Bhargava, S.C. (2003) 'Child and adolescent survivors of suicide.' *Crisis 24,* 1, 4–6.

10. Brent, D.A., Moritz, G., Bridge, J., Perper, J. and Canobbio, R. (1996) 'The impact of adolescent suicide on siblings and parents: A longitudinal follow-up.' *Suicide and Life-Threatening Behavior 26,* 3, 253–259.

11. Dyregrov, A. (2008) *Grief in Children: A Handbook for Adults,* 2nd edition. London: Jessica Kingsley Publishers.

    Dyregrov, K. (2009) 'The important role of the school following suicide: New research about the help and support wishes of the young bereaved.' *OMEGA – Journal of Death and Dying 59,* 2, 147–61.

    Silverman, P.R. (2000) *Death in Children's Lives.* New York, NY, and Oxford: Oxford University Press.

    Streeck-Fischer, A. and van der Kolk, B.A. (2000) 'Down will come baby, cradle and all: Diagnostic and therapeutic implications of chronic trauma on child development.' *Australian and New Zealand Journal of Psychiatry 34,* 6, 903–18.

12. Dyregrov, K. and Dyregrov, A. (2008) *Effective Grief and Bereavement Support: The Role of Family, Friends, Colleagues, Schools and Support Professionals.* London: Jessica Kingsley Publishers.

    Rose, A.J. (2002) 'Co-rumination in the friendships of girls and boys.' *Child Development 73,* 6, 4,1830–42.

    Rose, A.J., Carlson, E. and Waller, E.M. (2007) 'Prospective associations of co-rumination with friendship and emotional adjustment: Considering the socio-emotional trade-offs of co-rumination.' *Developmental Psychology 43,* 6, 4, 1019–31.

13. Dyregrov, A. (2008) *Grief in Children: A Handbook for Adults,* 2nd edition. London: Jessica Kingsley Publishers.

    Dyregrov, K. and Dyregrov, A. (2009) 'Helping the Family Following Suicide.' In B. Monroe and F. Kraus (eds) *Brief Interventions with Bereaved Children,* 2nd edition. Oxford: Oxford University Press.

CHAPTER 7

1. Dyregrov, K. and Dyregrov, A. (2008) *Effective Grief and Bereavement Support: The Role of Family, Friends, Colleagues, Schools and Support Professionals.* London: Jessica Kingsley Publishers.

2. Rose, A.J. (2002) 'Co-rumination in the friendships of girls and boys.' *Child Development 73,* 6, 4 1830–42.

    Rose, A.J., Carlson, E. and Waller, E.M. (2007) 'Prospective associations of co-rumination with friendship and emotional adjustment: Considering the socio-emotional trade-offs of co-rumination.' *Developmental Psychology 43,* 6, 4, 1019–31.

3. Dyregrov, K. (2003) *The Loss of a Child by Suicide, SIDS, and Accidents: Consequences, Needs and Provisions of Help*. Doctoral dissertation. Bergen, Norway: HEMIL, Faculty of Psychology, University of Bergen.

   Dyregrov, K. and Dyregrov, A. (2008) *Effective Grief and Bereavement Support: The Role of Family, Friends, Colleagues, Schools and Support Professionals*. London: Jessica Kingsley Publishers.

   Wertheimer, A. (2001) *A Special Scar: The Experiences of People Bereaved by Suicide*, 2nd revised edition. London: Taylor & Francis.

4. Jordan, J.R. and McIntosh, J.L. (eds) (2011) *Grief After Suicide: Understanding the Consequences and Caring for the Survivors*. New York, NY, and London: Routledge.

   Pennebaker, J.W. (1997) *Opening Up: The Healing Power of Expressing Emotion*. New York, NY: Guilford Press.

   Pennebaker, J.W. and Chung, C.K. (2007) 'Expressive Writing, Emotional Upheavals, and Health.' In H. Friedman and R. Silver (eds) *Handbook of Health Psychology*. New York, NY: Oxford University Press.

   Pennebaker, J.W. and Seagal, J.D. (1999) 'Forming a story: The health benefits of narrative.' *Journal of Clinical Psychology 55*, 10, 1243–54.

5. Bender, T., Nagy, G., Barna, I., Tefner, I., Kadas, E. and Geher, P. (2007) 'The effect of physical therapy on beta-endorphin levels.' *European Journal of Applied Physiology 100*, 4, 371–82.

6. Dyregrov, K. (2003) *The Loss of a Child by Suicide, SIDS, and Accidents: Consequences, Needs and Provisions of Help*. Doctoral dissertation. Bergen, Norway: HEMIL, Faculty of Psychology, University of Bergen.

   Dyregrov, K. and Dyregrov, A. (2008) *Effective Grief and Bereavement Support: The Role of Family, Friends, Colleagues, Schools and Support Professionals*. London: Jessica Kingsley Publishers.

7. Dyregrov, K. and Dyregrov, A. (2008) *Effective Grief and Bereavement Support: The Role of Family, Friends, Colleagues, Schools and Support Professionals*. London: Jessica Kingsley Publishers.

8. Dyregrov, K. and Dyregrov, A. (2008) *Effective Grief and Bereavement Support: The Role of Family, Friends, Colleagues, Schools and Support Professionals*. London: Jessica Kingsley Publishers.

CHAPTER 8

1. Dyregrov, K. (2003) *The Loss of a Child by Suicide, SIDS, and Accidents: Consequences, Needs and Provisions of Help*. Doctoral dissertation. Bergen, Norway: HEMIL, Faculty of Psychology, University of Bergen.

   Dyregrov, K. and Dyregrov, A. (2008) *Effective Grief and Bereavement Support: The Role of Family, Friends, Colleagues, Schools and Support Professionals*. London: Jessica Kingsley Publishers.

2. Dyregrov, K. (2003) *The Loss of a Child by Suicide, SIDS, and Accidents: Consequences, Needs and Provisions of Help*. Doctoral dissertation. Bergen, Norway: HEMIL, Faculty of Psychology, University of Bergen.

   Dyregrov, K. and Dyregrov, A. (2008) *Effective Grief and Bereavement Support: The Role of Family, Friends, Colleagues, Schools and Support Professionals*. London: Jessica Kingsley Publishers.

3. Dyregrov, K. and Dyregrov, A. (2008) *Effective Grief and Bereavement Support: The Role of Family, Friends, Colleagues, Schools and Support Professionals*. London: Jessica Kingsley Publishers.

4. Dyregrov, K. (2009) 'The important role of the school following suicide: New research about the help and support wishes of the young bereaved.' *OMEGA – Journal of Death and Dying 59*, 2, 147–61.

   Dyregrov, K. and Dyregrov, A. (2008) *Effective Grief and Bereavement Support: The Role of Family, Friends, Colleagues, Schools and Support Professionals*. London: Jessica Kingsley Publishers.
   Silverman, P.R. (2000) *Death in Children's Lives*. New York, NY, and Oxford: Oxford University Press.

5. Dyregrov, K. (2003) *The Loss of a Child by Suicide, SIDS, and Accidents. Consequences, Needs and Provisions of Help*. Doctoral dissertation. Bergen, Norway: HEMIL, Faculty of Psychology, University of Bergen.

Dyregrov, K. and Dyregrov, A. (2008) *Effective Grief and Bereavement Support: The Role of Family, Friends, Colleagues, Schools and Support Professionals.* London: Jessica Kingsley Publishers.

6. House, J.S. and Kahn, R.L. (1985) 'Measures and Concepts of Social Support.' In S. Cohen and S.L. Syme (eds) *Social Support and Health.* Orlando, FL: Academic Press.

7. Dyregrov, K. (2006) 'Experiences of social networks supporting traumatically bereaved.' *OMEGA – Journal of Death and Dying 52,* 4, 337–56.

    Dyregrov, K. and Dyregrov, A. (2008) *Effective Grief and Bereavement Support: The Role of Family, Friends, Colleagues, Schools and Support Professionals.* London: Jessica Kingsley Publishers.

8. Dyregrov, K. (2006) 'Experiences of social networks supporting traumatically bereaved.' *OMEGA – Journal of Death and Dying 52,* 4, 337–56.

    Dyregrov, K. and Dyregrov, A. (2008) *Effective Grief and Bereavement Support: The Role of Family, Friends, Colleagues, Schools and Support Professionals.* London: Jessica Kingsley Publishers.

9. Demi, A.S. and Howell, C. (1991) 'Hiding and healing: Resolving the suicide of a parent or sibling.' *Archives of Psychiatric Nursing 5,* 6, 350–6.

    Dyregrov, K. and Dyregrov, A. (2008) *Effective Grief and Bereavement Support: The Role of Family, Friends, Colleagues, Schools and Support Professionals.* London: Jessica Kingsley Publishers.

10. Dakof, G.A. and Taylor, S.E. (1990) 'Victims' perceptions of social support: What is helpful from whom?' *Journal of Personality and Social Psychology 58,* 1, 80–9.

    Demi, A.S. and Howell, C. (1991) 'Hiding and healing: Resolving the suicide of a parent or sibling.' *Archives of Psychiatric Nursing 5,* 6, 350–6.

    Dyregrov, K. and Dyregrov, A. (2008) *Effective Grief and Bereavement Support: The Role of Family, Friends, Colleagues, Schools and Support Professionals.* London: Jessica Kingsley Publishers.

11. Dyregrov, K. and Dyregrov, A. (2008) *Effective Grief and Bereavement Support: The Role of Family, Friends, Colleagues, Schools and Support Professionals.* London: Jessica Kingsley Publishers.

12. Dyregrov, K. and Dyregrov, A. (2008) *Effective Grief and Bereavement Support: The Role of Family, Friends, Colleagues, Schools and Support Professionals.* London: Jessica Kingsley Publishers.

CHAPTER 9

1. Dyregrov, K. and Dyregrov, A. (2008) *Effective Grief and Bereavement Support: The Role of Family, Friends, Colleagues, Schools and Support Professionals.* London: Jessica Kingsley Publishers.

    Feigelman, W., Gorman, B.S., Beal Chastain, K. and Jordan, J.R. (2008) 'Internet support groups for suicide survivors: A new mode for gaining bereavement assistance.' *OMEGA – Journal of Death and Dying 57,* 3, 217–43.

    Jordan J.R. (2001) 'Is suicide bereavement different? A reassessment of the literature.' *Suicide and Life-Threatening Behavior 31,* 1, 91–102.

    Jordan, J.R. and McIntosh, J.L. (eds) (2011) *Grief After Suicide: Understanding the Consequences and Caring for the Survivors.* New York, NY, and London: Routledge.

    Wertheimer, A. (2001) *A Special Scar: The Experiences of People Bereaved by Suicide,* 2nd revised edition. London: Taylor & Francis.

2. Jordan, J.R. and McIntosh, J.L. (eds) (2011) *Grief After Suicide: Understanding the Consequences and Caring for the Survivors.* New York, NY, and London: Routledge.

3. Jordan, J.R. and McIntosh, J.L. (eds) (2011) *Grief After Suicide: Understanding the Consequences and Caring for the Survivors.* New York, NY, and London: Routledge.

4. Jordan, J.R. and McIntosh, J.L. (eds) (2011) *Grief After Suicide: Understanding the Consequences and Caring for the Survivors.* New York, NY, and London: Routledge.

5. Jordan, J.R. and McIntosh, J.L. (eds) (2011) *Grief After Suicide: Understanding the Consequences and Caring for the Survivors.* New York, NY, and London: Routledge.

6. Feigelman, W., Gorman, B.S., Beal Chastain, K. and Jordan, J.R. (2008) 'Internet support groups for suicide survivors: A new mode for gaining bereavement assistance.' *OMEGA – Journal of Death and Dying 57,* 3, 217–43.

Jordan, J.R. and McIntosh, J.L. (eds) (2011) *Grief After Suicide: Understanding the Consequences and Caring for the Survivors.* New York, NY, and London: Routledge.

7. Dyregrov, K. (2003) *The Loss of a Child by Suicide, SIDS, and Accidents: Consequences, Needs and Provisions of Help.* Doctoral dissertation. Bergen, Norway: HEMIL, Faculty of Psychology, University of Bergen.

Dyregrov, K. and Dyregrov, A. (2008) *Effective Grief and Bereavement Support: The Role of Family, Friends, Colleagues, Schools and Support Professionals.* London: Jessica Kingsley Publishers.

Dyregrov, K. and Dyregrov, A. (2009) 'Helping the Family Following Suicide.' In B. Monroe and F. Kraus (eds) *Brief Interventions with Bereaved Children,* 2nd edition. Oxford: Oxford University Press.

Jordan, J.R. and McIntosh, J.L. (eds) (2011) *Grief After Suicide: Understanding the Consequences and Caring for the Survivors.* New York, NY, and London: Routledge.

Wertheimer, A. (2001) *A Special Scar: The Experiences of People Bereaved by Suicide,* 2nd revised edition. London: Taylor & Francis.

CHAPTER 10

1. Dyregrov, K. (in press) 'What do we know about needs for help after suicide in different parts of the world? A phenomenological perspective.' Available at http://ifp.es.nyu.edu/?p=120510, accessed 19 July 2011.

Jordan, J.R. and McIntosh, J.L. (eds) (2011) *Grief After Suicide: Understanding the Consequences and Caring for the Survivors.* New York, NY, and London: Routledge.

McMenamy J., Jordan J. and Mitchell A. (2008) 'What do survivors tell us they need? Results from a pilot study.' *Suicide and Life-Threatening Behavior 38,* 4, 375–89.

Provini, C., Everett, J.R. and Pfeffer, C.R. (2000) 'Adults mourning suicide: Self-reported concerns about bereavement, needs for assistance, and help-seeking behavior.' *Death Studies 24,* 1, 1–9.

Wilson, A. and Clark, S. (2005) *South Australian Suicide Postvention Project.* Report to Mental Health Services, Department of Health.

2. Dyregrov, K. (2002) 'Assistance from local authorities versus survivors' needs for support after suicide.' *Death Studies 26,* 8, 647–69.

Dyregrov, K. and Dyregrov, A. (2008) *Effective Grief and Bereavement Support: The Role of Family, Friends, Colleagues, Schools and Support Professionals.* London: Jessica Kingsley Publishers.

3. Dyregrov, K. (2002) 'Assistance from local authorities versus survivors' needs for support after suicide.' *Death Studies 26,* 8, 647–69.

Dyregrov, K. (in press) 'What do we know about needs for help after suicide in different parts of the world? A phenomenological perspective.' Available at http://ifp.es.nyu.edu/?p=120510, accessed 19 July 2011.

Jordan, J.R. and McIntosh, J.L. (eds) (2011) *Grief After Suicide: Understanding the Consequences and Caring for the Survivors.* New York, NY, and London: Routledge.

Provini, C., Everett, J.R. and Pfeffer, C.R. (2000) 'Adults mourning suicide: Self-reported concerns about bereavement, needs for assistance, and help-seeking behavior.' *Death Studies 24,* 1, 1–9.

Wertheimer, A. (2001) *A Special Scar: The Experiences of People Bereaved by Suicide,* 2nd revised edition. London: Taylor & Francis.

4. Dyregrov, K. (in press) 'What do we know about needs for help after suicide in different parts of the world? A phenomenological perspective.' Available at http://ifp.es.nyu.edu/?p=120510, accessed 19 July 2011.

Dyregrov, K. and Dyregrov, A. (2005) 'Siblings after suicide: "The forgotten bereaved".' *Suicide and Life-Threatening Behavior 35,* 6, 714–24.

Dyregrov, K. and Dyregrov, A. (2009) 'Helping the Family Following Suicide.' In B. Monroe and F. Kraus (eds) *Brief Interventions with Bereaved Children,* 2nd edition. Oxford: Oxford University Press.

5. Dyregrov, K. (2003) *The Loss of a Child by Suicide, SIDS, and Accidents: Consequences, Needs and Provisions of Help.* Doctoral dissertation. Bergen, Norway: HEMIL, Faculty of Psychology, University of Bergen.

Dyregrov, K. (2011) 'International Perspectives on Suicide Bereavement: Suicide Survivors and Postvention in Norway.' In J.R. Jordan and J.L. McIntosh (eds) *Understanding the Consequences and Caring for the Survivors.* New York, NY: Routledge.

Dyregrov, K. and Dyregrov, A. (2008) *Effective Grief and Bereavement Support: The Role of Family, Friends, Colleagues, Schools and Support Professionals.* London: Jessica Kingsley Publishers.

6. Murray, J.A., Terry, D.J., Vance, J.C., Battistutta, D. and Connolly, Y. (2000) 'Effects of a program of intervention on parental distress following infant death.' *Death Studies 24,* 4, 275–305.

7. Amaya-Jackson, L., Davidson, J.R., Hughes, D.C., Swartz, M. *et al.* (1999) 'Functional impairment and utilization of services associated with posttraumatic stress in the community.' *Journal of Traumatic Stress 12,* 4, 709–24.

Provini, C., Everett, J.R. and Pfeffer, C.R. (2000) 'Adults mourning suicide: Self-reported concerns about bereavement, needs for assistance, and help-seeking behavior.' *Death Studies 24,* 1, 1–9.

8. Provini, C., Everett, J.R. and Pfeffer, C.R. (2000) 'Adults mourning suicide: Self-reported concerns about bereavement, needs for assistance, and help-seeking behavior.' *Death Studies 24,* 1, 1–9.

9. Pfeffer, C.R., Martins, P., Mann, J., Sunkenberg, R.N. *et al.* (1997) 'Child survivors of suicide: Psychosocial characteristics.' *Journal of the American Academy of Child and Adolescent Psychiatry 36,* 1, 65–74.

10. Murphy, S.A. (2000) 'The use of research findings in bereavement programs: A case study.' *Death Studies 24,* 7, 585–602.

11. Bryant, R.A., Harvey, A.G., Dang, S.T., Sackville, T. *et al.* (1998) 'Treatment of acute stress disorder: A comparison of cognitive-behavioral therapy and supportive counseling.' *Journal of Consulting and Clinical Psychology 66,* 5, 862–6.

12. Murphy, S.A. (2000) 'The use of research findings in bereavement programs: A case study.' *Death Studies 24,* 7, 585–602.

Murray, J.A., Terry, D.J., Vance, J.C., Battistutta, D. and Connolly, Y. (2000) 'Effects of a program of intervention on parental distress following infant death.' *Death Studies 24,* 4, 275–305.

13. Neimeyer, R.A., Baldwin, S.A. and Gilles, J. (2006) 'Continuing bonds and reconstructing meaning: Mitigating complications in bereavement.' *Death Studies 30,* 8, 715–38.

Shear, K., Frank, E., Houck, P.R. and Reynolds, C.F. (2005) 'Treatment of complicated grief.' *Journal of the American Medical Association 293,* 21, 2601–8.

Stroebe, M.S., Hansson R.O., Schut, H. and Stroebe, W. (2008) 'Bereavement Research: 21st-Century Prospects.' In M.S. Stroebe, R.O. Hansson, H. Schut and W. Stroebe (eds) *Handbook of Bereavement Research and Practice: Advances in Theory and Intervention.* Washington, DC: American Psychological Association.

14. Dyregrov, A. (2010) *Supporting Traumatized Children and Teenagers.* London: Jessica Kingsley Publishers.

Dyregrov, K. and Dyregrov, A. (2008) *Effective Grief and Bereavement Support: The Role of Family, Friends, Colleagues, Schools and Support Professionals.* London: Jessica Kingsley Publishers.

Dyregrov, K. and Dyregrov, A. (2009) 'Helping the Family Following Suicide.' In B. Monroe and F. Kraus (eds) *Brief Interventions with Bereaved Children,* 2nd edition. Oxford: Oxford University Press.

Jordan, J.R. and McIntosh, J.L. (eds) (2011) *Grief After Suicide: Understanding the Consequences and Caring for the Survivors.* New York, NY, and London: Routledge.

15. Dyregrov, A. (2010) *Supporting Traumatized Children and Teenagers.* London: Jessica Kingsley Publishers.

Dyregrov, K. and Dyregrov, A. (2008) *Effective Grief and Bereavement Support: The Role of Family, Friends, Colleagues, Schools and Support Professionals.* London: Jessica Kingsley Publishers.

Dyregrov, K. and Dyregrov, A. (2009) 'Helping the Family Following Suicide.' In B. Monroe and F. Kraus (eds) *Brief Interventions with Bereaved Children,* 2nd edition. Oxford: Oxford University Press.

Jordan, J.R. and McIntosh, J.L. (eds) (2011) *Grief After Suicide: Understanding the Consequences and Caring for the Survivors.* New York, NY, and London: Routledge.

16. Dyregrov, K. and Dyregrov, A. (2005) 'Siblings after suicide: "The forgotten bereaved".' *Suicide and Life-Threatening Behavior 35,* 6, 714–24.

Dyregrov, K. and Dyregrov, A. (2009) 'Helping the Family Following Suicide.' In B. Monroe and F. Kraus (eds) *Brief Interventions with Bereaved Children,* 2nd edition. Oxford: Oxford University Press.

Jordan, J.R. and McIntosh, J.L. (eds) (2011) *Grief After Suicide: Understanding the Consequences and Caring for the Survivors.* New York, NY, and London: Routledge.

Rakic, A.S. (1992) *Sibling Survivors of Adolescent Suicide.* Doctoral dissertation. Alameda, CA: The California School of Professional Psychology, Berkeley/Alameda.

17. Jordan, J.R. and McIntosh, J.L. (eds) (2011) *Grief After Suicide: Understanding the Consequences and Caring for the Survivors.* New York, NY, and London: Routledge.

18. Dyregrov, K. and Dyregrov, A. (2008) *Effective Grief and Bereavement Support: The Role of Family, Friends, Colleagues, Schools and Support Professionals.* London: Jessica Kingsley Publishers.

19. Archer, J. (2008) 'Theories of Grief: Past, Present, and Future Perspectives.' In M.S. Stroebe, R.O. Hansson, H. Schut and W. Stroebe (eds) *Handbook of Bereavement Research and Practice: Advances in Theory and Intervention.* Washington, DC: American Psychological Association.

Bonanno, G., Mihalecz, M. and LeJeune, J. (1999) 'The core emotion themes of conjugal loss.' *Motivation and Emotion 23,* 3, 175–201.

Stroebe, M.S., Hansson R.O., Schut, H. and Stroebe, W. (2008) 'Bereavement Research: 21st Century Prospects.' In M.S. Stroebe, R.O. Hansson, H. Schut and W. Stroebe (eds) *Handbook of Bereavement Research and Practice: Advances in Theory and Intervention.* Washington, DC: American Psychological Association.

Stroebe, M.S. and Schut, H. (1999) 'The dual process model of coping with bereavement: Rationale and description.' *Death Studies 23,* 3, 197–224.

20. Dyregrov, K. (2003) *The Loss of a Child by Suicide, SIDS, and Accidents: Consequences, Needs and Provisions of Help.* Doctoral dissertation. Bergen, Norway: HEMIL, Faculty of Psychology, University of Bergen.

Jordan, J.R. and McIntosh, J.L. (eds) (2011) *Grief After Suicide: Understanding the Consequences and Caring for the Survivors.* New York, NY, and London: Routledge.

21. Bryant, R.A., Harvey, A.G., Dang, S.T., Sackville, T. *et al.* (1998) 'Treatment of acute stress disorder: A comparison of cognitive-behavioral therapy and supportive counseling.' *Journal of Consulting and Clinical Psychology 66,* 5, 862–6.

22. Dyregrov, K. and Dyregrov, A. (2008) *Effective Grief and Bereavement Support: The Role of Family, Friends, Colleagues, Schools and Support Professionals.* London: Jessica Kingsley Publishers.

23. Shear, K., Frank, E., Houck, P.R. and Reynolds, C.F. (2005) 'Treatment of complicated grief.' *Journal of the American Medical Association 293,* 21, 2601–8.

24. Jordan, J.R. and McIntosh, J.L. (eds) (2011) *Grief After Suicide: Understanding the Consequences and Caring for the Survivors.* New York, NY, and London: Routledge.

Nadeau, J.W. (1997) *Families Making Sense of Death.* Thousand Oaks, CA: Sage Publications.

25. Dyregrov, K. (2002) 'Assistance from local authorities versus survivors' needs for support after suicide.' *Death Studies 26,* 8, 647–69.

26. Dyregrov, K. (2002) 'Assistance from local authorities versus survivors' needs for support after suicide.' *Death Studies 26,* 8, 647–69.

CHAPTER 11

1. Boerner, K. and Heckhausen, J. (2003) 'To have and have not: Adaptive bereavement by transforming mental ties to the deceased.' *Death Studies 27*, 3, 199–226.

2. Bowlby, J. (1961) 'Processes of mourning.' *International Journal of Psychoanalysis 42*, 317–40.
   Parkes, C.M. (1998) 'Traditional models and theories of grief.' *Bereavement Care 17*, 2, 21–3.

3. Worden, J.W. (1982) *Grief Counseling and Grief Therapy.* New York, NY: Springer Publishing Company.

4. Bonanno, G., Mihalecz, M. and LeJeune, J. (1999) 'The core emotion themes of conjugal loss.' *Motivation and Emotion 23*, 3, 175–201.

5. Stroebe, M.S., Hansson R.O., Schut, H. and Stroebe, W. (2008) 'Bereavement Research: 21st-Century Prospects.' In M.S. Stroebe, R.O. Hansson, H. Schut and W. Stroebe (eds) *Handbook of Bereavement Research and Practice: Advances in Theory and Intervention.* Washington, DC: American Psychological Association.

6. Archer, J. (2008) 'Theories of Grief: Past, Present, and Future Perspectives.' In M.S. Stroebe, R.O. Hansson, H. Schut and W. Stroebe (eds) *Handbook of Bereavement Research and Practice: Advances in Theory and Intervention.* Washington, DC: American Psychological Association.
   Stroebe, M.S. and Schut, H. (1999) 'The dual process model of coping with bereavement: Rationale and description.' *Death Studies 23*, 3, 197–224.

7. Stroebe, M.S. and Schut, H. (1999) 'The dual process model of coping with bereavement: Rationale and description.' *Death Studies 23*, 3, 197–224.

8. Dyregrov, K. and Dyregrov, A. (2008) *Effective Grief and Bereavement Support: The Role of Family, Friends, Colleagues, Schools and Support Professionals.* London: Jessica Kingsley Publishers.

9. Neimeyer, R.A. (2000) 'Searching for the meaning: Grief therapy and the process of reconstruction.' *Death Studies 24*, 6, 541–58.
   Neimeyer, R.A. (ed.) (2001) *Meaning Reconstruction and the Experience of Loss.* Washington, DC: American Psychological Association.

10. Boerner, K. and Heckhausen, J. (2003) 'To have and have not: Adaptive bereavement by transforming mental ties to the deceased.' *Death Studies 27*, 3, 199–226.

11. Dyregrov, K. and Dyregrov, A. (2008) *Effective Grief and Bereavement Support: The Role of Family, Friends, Colleagues, Schools and Support Professionals.* London: Jessica Kingsley Publishers.
   Riches, G. and Dawson, P. (1996) 'Making stories and taking stories: Methodological reflections on researching grief and marital tension following the death of a child.' *British Journal of Guidance and Counselling 24*, 3, 357–65.
   Rose, A.J. (2002) 'Co-rumination in the friendships of girls and boys.' *Child Development 73*, 6, 1830–42.
   Rose, A.J., Carlson, E. and Waller, E.M. (2007) 'Prospective associations of co-rumination with friendship and emotional adjustment: Considering the socio-emotional trade-offs of co-rumination.' *Developmental Psychology 43*, 4, 1019–31.

12. Dyregrov, A. and Dyregrov, K. (1999) 'Long-term impact of sudden infant death: A 12- to 15-year follow-up.' *Death Studies 23*, 7, 635–61.

13. Murphy, S.A., Johnson, L.C. and Lohan, J. (2002) 'The aftermath of the violent death of a child: An integration of the assessments of parents' mental distress and PTSD during the first 5 years of bereavement.' *Journal of Loss and Trauma 7*, 3, 203–22.

14. Janoff-Bulman, R. (1992) *Shattered Assumptions: Towards a New Psychology of Trauma.* New York, NY: The Free Press.

15. Giddens, A. (1991) *Modernity and Self-Identity.* Cambridge: Polity Press.

16. Berger, P.L. and Luckmann, T. (1966) *The Social Construction of Reality: A Treatise in the Sociology of Knowledge.* Garden City, NY: Doubleday.

17. Joseph, S. and Linley, P.A. (2005) 'Positive adjustment to threatening events: An organismic valuing theory of growth through adversity.' *Review of General Psychology 9*, 3, 262–80.

Tedeschi, R.G. and Calhoun, L.G. (1995) *Trauma and Transformation: Growing in the Aftermath of Suffering*. London: Sage Publications.

Tedeschi, R.G. and Calhoun, L.G. (2004) 'Posttraumatic growth: Conceptual foundations and empirical evidence.' *Psychological Inquiry 15*, 1, 1–18.

Tedeschi, R.G., Park, C. and Calhoun, L.G. (1998) *Posttraumatic Growth: Positive Changes in the Aftermath of Crisis*. Mahwah, NJ: Erlbaum.

18. Davis, C.G., Wohl, M.J.A. and Verberg, N. (2007) 'Profiles of posttraumatic growth following an unjust loss.' *Death Studies 31*, 8, 693–712.

Dyregrov, K. (2003) *The Loss of a Child by Suicide, SIDS, and Accidents: Consequences, Needs and Provisions of Help*. Doctoral dissertation. Bergen, Norway: HEMIL, Faculty of Psychology, University of Bergen.

Dyregrov, K. and Dyregrov, A. (2008) *Effective Grief and Bereavement Support: The Role of Family, Friends, Colleagues, Schools and Support Professionals*. London: Jessica Kingsley Publishers.

Feigelman, W., Jordan, J.R. and Gorman, B.S. (2009) 'Personal growth after a suicide loss: Cross-sectional findings suggest growth after loss may be associated with better health among survivors.' *OMEGA – Journal of Death and Dying 59*, 3, 181–202.

Tedeschi, R.G., Park, C. and Calhoun, L.G. (1998) *Posttraumatic Growth: Positive Changes in the Aftermath of Crisis*. Mahwah, NJ: Erlbaum.

19. Davis, C.G., Wohl, M.J.A. and Verberg, N. (2007) 'Profiles of posttraumatic growth following an unjust loss.' *Death Studies 31*, 8, 693–712.

Feigelman, W., Jordan, J.R. and Gorman, B.S. (2009) 'Personal growth after a suicide loss: Cross-sectional findings suggest growth after loss may be associated with better health among survivors.' *OMEGA – Journal of Death and Dying 59*, 3, 181–202.

Wolchik, S.A., Coxe, S., Tein, J-Y., Sandler, I.N. and Ayers, T.S. (2008) 'Six-year longitudinal predictors of posttraumatic growth in parentally bereaved adolescents and young adults.' *OMEGA – Journal of Death and Dying 58*, 2, 107–28.

20. Feigelman, W., Jordan, J.R. and Gorman, B.S. (2009) 'Personal growth after a suicide loss: Cross-sectional findings suggest growth after loss may be associated with better health among survivors.' *OMEGA – Journal of Death and Dying 59*, 3, 181–202.

Helgeson, V.S., Reynolds, K.A. and Tomich, P.L. (2006) 'A meta-analytic review of benefit finding and growth.' *Journal of Consulting and Clinical Psychology 74*, 5, 797–816.

Wolchik, S.A., Coxe, S., Tein, J-Y., Sandler, I.N. and Ayers, T.S. (2008) 'Six-year longitudinal predictors of posttraumatic growth in parentally bereaved adolescents and young adults.' *OMEGA – Journal of Death and Dying 58*, 2, 107–28.

CHAPTER 12

1. Blair-West, G.W., Cantor, C.H., Mellsop, G.W. and Eyeson-Annan, M.L. (1994) 'Lifetime suicide risk in major depression: Sex and age determinants.' *Journal of Affective Disorders 55*, 2–3, 171–178.

2. Inskip, H.M., Harris, E.C. and Barraclough, B. (1998) 'Lifetime risk of suicide for affective disorder, alcoholism and schizophrenia.' *British Journal of Psychiatry 172*, 1, 35–37.

Palmer, B.A., Pankratz, V.S. and Bostwick, J.M. (2005) 'The lifetime risk of suicide in schizophrenia: A re-examination.' *Archives of General Psychiatry 62*, 3, 247–253.

3. Hawton, K. (ed.) (2005) *Prevention and Treatment of Suicidal Behaviour: From Science to Practice*. Oxford: Oxford University Press.

4. Rudd, M.D., Joiner, T. and Rajab, M.H. (2001) *Treating Suicidal Behavior: An Effective, Time-Limited Approach*. New York, NY: Guilford Press.

5. Rudd, M.D., Trotter, D.R.M. and Williams, B. (2009) 'Psychological Theories of Suicidal Behaviour.' In D. Wasserman and C. Wasserman (eds) *Suicidology and Suicide Prevention: A Global Perspective*. New York, NY: Oxford University Press.

6. Schotte, D.E. and Clum, G.A. (1987) 'Problem-solving skills in suicidal psychiatric patients.' *Journal of Consulting and Clinical Psychology 55*, 1, 49–54.

7. Williams, M. (2001) *Suicide and Attempted Suicide: Understanding the Cry of Pain.* London: Penguin.

8. Rudd, M.D., Trotter, D.R.M. and Williams, B. (2009) 'Psychological Theories of Suicidal Behaviour.' In D. Wasserman and C. Wasserman (eds) *Suicidology and Suicide Prevention: A Global Perspective.* New York, NY: Oxford University Press.

   Williams, M. (2001) *Suicide and Attempted Suicide: Understanding the Cry of Pain.* London: Penguin.

9. Shneidman, E. (1985) *Definition of Suicide.* New York, NY: Wiley.

10. Beck, A.T., Brown, G., Berchick, R.J., Stewart, B.L. and Steer, R.A. (1990) 'Relationship between hopelessness and ultimate suicide: A replication with psychiatric outpatients.' *American Journal of Psychiatry 147*, 2, 190–5.

11. Leenaars, A.A. (2004) *Psychotherapy with Suicidal People: A Person-Centred Approach.* Chichester: John Wiley & Sons.

    Michel, K., Dey, P., Stadler, K. and Valach, L. (2004) 'Therapist sensitivity towards emotional life-career issues and the working alliance with suicide attempters.' *Archives of Suicide Research 8*, 3, 203–13.

12. Shneidman, E.S. (2004) *Autopsy of a Suicidal Mind.* Oxford: Oxford University Press. Orbach, I., Mikulincer, M., Gilboa-Schechtman, E. and Sirota, P. (2003) 'Mental pain and its relationship to suicidality and life meaning.' *Suicide and Life-Threatening Behavior 33*, 3, 231–41.

13. Beck, A.T., Brown, G., Berchick, R.J., Stewart, B.L. and Steer, R.A. (1990) 'Relationship between hopelessness and ultimate suicide: A replication with psychiatric outpatients.' *American Journal of Psychiatry 147*, 2, 190–5.

14. Rudd, M.D., Joiner, T. and Rajab, M.H. (2001) *Treating Suicidal Behavior: An Effective, Time-Limited Approach.* New York, NY: Guilford Press.

15. Rudd, M.D., Joiner, T. and Rajab, M.H. (2001) *Treating Suicidal Behavior: An Effective, Time-Limited Approach.* New York, NY: Guilford Press.

16. Hawton, K. (ed.) (2005) *Prevention and Treatment of Suicidal Behaviour: From Science to Practice.* Oxford: Oxford University Press.

17. Rudd, M.D., Trotter, D.R.M. and Williams, B. (2009) 'Psychological Theories of Suicidal Behaviour.' In D. Wasserman and C. Wasserman (eds) *Suicidology and Suicide Prevention: A Global Perspective.* New York, NY: Oxford University Press.

18. Williams, M. (2001) *Suicide and Attempted Suicide: Understanding the Cry of Pain.* London: Penguin.

19. Rudd, M.D., Joiner, T. and Rajab, M.H. (2001) *Treating Suicidal Behavior: An Effective, Time-Limited Approach.* New York, NY: Guilford Press.

USEFUL RESOURCES

1. Dyregrov, K. (2009) 'The important role of the school following suicide: New research about the help and support wishes of the young bereaved.' *OMEGA – Journal of Death and Dying 59*, 2, 147–161.

   Dyregrov, K. (2009) 'How do the young suicide survivors wish to be met by psychologists? A user study.' *OMEGA – Journal of Death and Dying 59*, 3, 221–238.

Index